RESTORED

A STUDY ON THE BOOK OF JOEL

TIFFANY DICKERSON

STUDY SUGGESTIONS

We believe that the Bible is true, trustworthy, and timeless and that it is vitally important for all believers. These study suggestions are intended to help you more effectively study Scripture as you seek to know and love God through His Word.

SUGGESTED STUDY TOOLS

- A Bible

- A double-spaced, printed copy of the Scripture passages that this study covers. You can use a website like *www.biblegateway.com* to copy the text of a passage and print out a double-spaced copy to be able to mark on easily

- A journal to write notes or prayers

- Pens, colored pencils, and highlighters

- A dictionary to look up unfamiliar words

HOW TO USE THIS STUDY

Begin your study time in prayer. Ask God to reveal Himself to you, to help you understand what you are reading, and to transform you with His Word (Psalm 119:18).

Before you read what is written in each day of the study itself, read the assigned passages of Scripture for that day. Use your double-spaced copy to circle, underline, highlight, draw arrows, and mark in any way you would like to help you dig deeper as you work through a passage.

Read the daily written content provided for the current study day.

Answer the questions that appear at the end of each study day.

HOW TO STUDY THE BIBLE

The inductive method provides tools for deeper and more intentional Bible study. To study the Bible inductively, work through the steps below after reading background information on the book.

OBSERVATION & COMPREHENSION
Key question: What does the text say?

After reading the daily Scripture in its entirety at least once, begin working with smaller portions of the Scripture. Read a passage of Scripture repetitively, and then mark the following items in the text:

- Key or repeated words and ideas
- Key themes
- Transition words (Ex: therefore, but, because, if/then, likewise, etc.)
- Lists
- Comparisons and contrasts
- Commands
- Unfamiliar words (look these up in a dictionary)
- Questions you have about the text

INTERPRETATION
Key question: What does the text mean?

Once you have annotated the text, work through the following steps to help you interpret its meaning:

- Read the passage in other versions for a better understanding of the text.
- Read cross-references to help interpret Scripture with Scripture.
- Paraphrase or summarize the passage to check for understanding.
- Identify how the text reflects the metanarrative of Scripture, which is the story of creation, fall, redemption, and restoration.
- Read trustworthy commentaries if you need further insight into the meaning of the passage.

3 APPLICATION
Key Question: How should the truth of this passage change me?

Bible study is not merely an intellectual pursuit. The truths about God, ourselves, and the gospel that we discover in Scripture should produce transformation in our hearts and lives. Answer the following questions as you consider what you have learned in your study:

- What attributes of God's character are revealed in the passage?

    Consider places where the text directly states the character of God, as well as how His character is revealed through His words and actions.

- What do I learn about myself in light of who God is?

    Consider how you fall short of God's character, how the text reveals your sin nature, and what it says about your new identity in Christ.

- How should this truth change me?

    A passage of Scripture may contain direct commands telling us what to do or warnings about sins to avoid in order to help us grow in holiness. Other times our application flows out of seeing ourselves in light of God's character. As we pray and reflect on how God is calling us to change in light of His Word, we should be asking questions like, "How should I pray for God to change my heart?" and "What practical steps can I take toward cultivating habits of holiness?"

THE ATTRIBUTES OF GOD

ETERNAL

God has no beginning and no end. He always was, always is, and always will be.

HAB. 1:12 / REV. 1:8 / IS. 41:4

FAITHFUL

God is incapable of anything but fidelity. He is loyally devoted to His plan and purpose.

2 TIM. 2:13 / DEUT. 7:9
HEB. 10:23

GOOD

God is pure; there is no defilement in Him. He is unable to sin, and all He does is good.

GEN. 1:31 / PS. 34:8 / PS. 107:1

GRACIOUS

God is kind, giving us gifts and benefits we do not deserve.

2 KINGS 13:23 / PS. 145:8
IS. 30:18

HOLY

God is undefiled and unable to be in the presence of defilement. He is sacred and set-apart.

REV. 4:8 / LEV. 19:2 / HAB. 1:13

INCOMPREHENSIBLE & TRANSCENDENT

God is high above and beyond human understanding. He is unable to be fully known.

PS. 145:3 / IS. 55:8-9
ROM. 11:33-36

IMMUTABLE

God does not change. He is the same yesterday, today, and tomorrow.

1 SAM. 15:29 / ROM. 11:29
JAMES 1:17

INFINITE

God is limitless. He exhibits all of His attributes perfectly and boundlessly.

ROM. 11:33-36 / IS. 40:28
PS. 147:5

JEALOUS

God is desirous of receiving the praise and affection He rightly deserves.

EX. 20:5 / DEUT. 4:23-24
JOSH. 24:19

JUST

God governs in perfect justice. He acts in accordance with justice. In Him, there is no wrongdoing or dishonesty.

IS. 61:8 / DEUT. 32:4 / PS. 146:7-9

LOVING

God is eternally, enduringly, steadfastly loving and affectionate. He does not forsake or betray His covenant love.

JN. 3:16 / EPH. 2:4-5 / 1 JN. 4:16

MERCIFUL

God is compassionate, withholding from us the wrath that we deserve.

TITUS 3:5 / PS. 25:10
LAM. 3:22-23

OMNIPOTENT

God is all-powerful; His strength is unlimited.

MAT. 19:26 / JOB 42:1-2
JER. 32:27

OMNIPRESENT

God is everywhere; His presence is near and permeating.

PROV. 15:3 / PS. 139:7-10
JER. 23:23-24

OMNISCIENT

God is all-knowing; there is nothing unknown to Him.

PS. 147:4 / 1 JN. 3:20
HEB. 4:13

PATIENT

God is long-suffering and enduring. He gives ample opportunity for people to turn toward Him.

ROM. 2:4 / 2 PET. 3:9 / PS. 86:15

SELF-EXISTENT

God was not created but exists by His power alone.

PS. 90:1-2 / JN. 1:4 / JN. 5:26

SELF-SUFFICIENT

God has no needs and depends on nothing, but everything depends on God.

IS. 40:28-31 / ACTS 17:24-25
PHIL. 4:19

SOVEREIGN

God governs over all things; He is in complete control.

COL. 1:17 / PS. 24:1-2
1 CHRON. 29:11-12

TRUTHFUL

God is our measurement of what is fact. By Him we are able to discern true and false.

JN. 3:33 / ROM. 1:25 / JN. 14:6

WISE

God is infinitely knowledgeable and is judicious with His knowledge.

IS. 46:9-10 / IS. 55:9 / PROV. 3:19

WRATHFUL

God stands in opposition to all that is evil. He enacts judgment according to His holiness, righteousness, and justice.

PS. 69:24 / JN. 3:36 / ROM. 1:18

TIMELINE OF SCRIPTURE

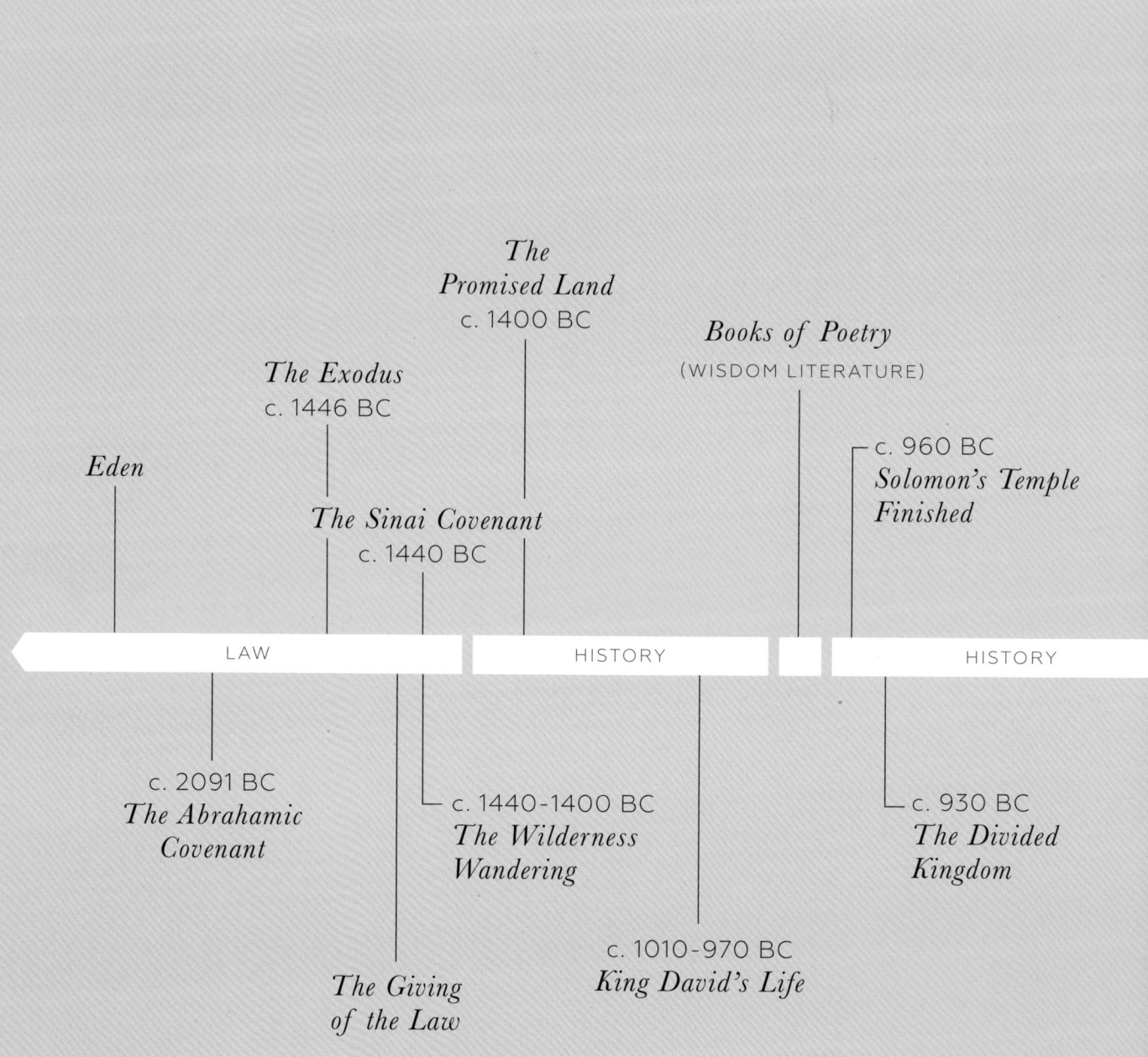

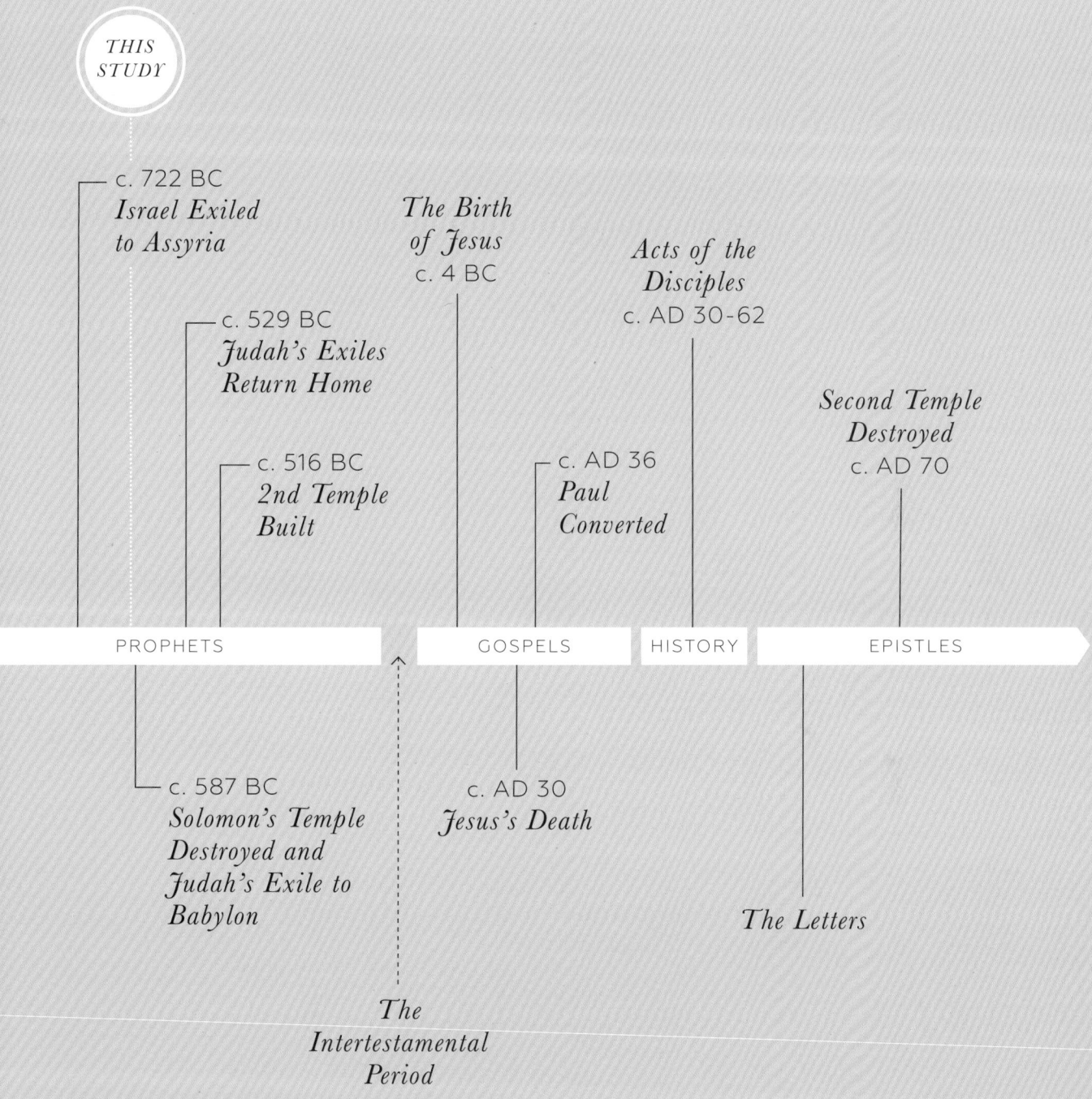

TIMELINE OF SCRIPTURE

METANARRATIVE OF SCRIPTURE

Creation

In the beginning, God created the universe. He made the world and everything in it. He created humans in His own image to be His representatives on the earth.

Fall

The first humans, Adam and Eve, disobeyed God by eating from the fruit of the Tree of Knowledge of Good and Evil. Their disobedience impacted the whole world. The punishment for sin is death, and because of Adam's original sin, all humans are sinful and condemned to death.

Redemption

God sent His Son to become a human and redeem His people. Jesus Christ lived a sinless life but died on the cross to pay the penalty for sin. He resurrected from the dead and ascended into heaven. All who put their faith in Jesus are saved from death and freely receive the gift of eternal life.

Restoration

One day, Jesus Christ will return again and restore all that sin destroyed. He will usher in a new heaven and new earth where all who trust in Him will live eternally with glorified bodies in the presence of God.

> "JOEL'S MESSAGE STANDS THE TEST OF TIME FOR READERS TO LEARN FROM THE PAST AND PREPARE FOR THE FUTURE.

Evan
Evan

IN THIS STUDY

WEEK ONE
DAY ONE — 18
SCRIPTURE MEMORY — 48
WEEK ONE REFLECTION — 50

WEEK TWO
DAY ONE — 52
SCRIPTURE MEMORY — 82
WEEK TWO REFLECTION — 84

WEEK THREE
DAY ONE — 86
SCRIPTURE MEMORY — 114
WEEK THREE REFLECTION — 116

EXTRAS
STUDY SUGGESTIONS — 2
HOW TO STUDY THE BIBLE — 4
THE ATTRIBUTES OF GOD — 6
TIMELINE OF SCRIPTURE — 8
METANARRATIVE OF SCRIPTURE — 10
HOW TO READ THE PROPHETS — 14
WHAT IS THE GOSPEL? — 118

HOW TO READ THE PROPHETS

Before you begin, remember that Joel is a prophetic book. Understanding the genre of prophecy will help as you approach your study. The Old Testament prophetic books are grouped by the Major Prophets and the Minor Prophets. This is simply based on length. Each prophet received the Word of God and was tasked with sharing God's message with a particular audience—typically, the Israelites, though some prophetic books address other nations as well. As God's messengers, the prophets called out the sin of the nation, announced judgment, called for repentance, and even proclaimed the Messiah's first and second coming.

Prophetic books are filled with dramatic and vivid word imagery that communicates the truth of God. Inanimate objects may take on lifelike abilities to point to a specific truth. Or an animal could represent a nation and its impending judgment. Figurative language will point you to metaphors and similes to help you better understand God's message.

Prophetic books often cover various time periods. Some judgments and blessings were poured out as a near fulfillment during the time of the prophet's initial message, while others find their fulfillment in Christ and the church age. Others will not occur until Christ returns and sets up the glorious new heaven and new earth. Take your time as you read this prophetic book; ponder the imagery, learn from the judgments, consider the message God has for His people, and examine your heart's posture toward Christ.

Studying the Prophets is a worthwhile exercise as you draw closer to the heart of God. The Bible tells us, "All Scripture is inspired by God and is profitable for teaching, for rebuking, for correcting, for training in righteousness, so that the man of God may be complete, equipped for every good work" (2 Timothy 3:16–17). May this time in the Word encourage your walk with the Lord and make you more like Christ.

> STUDYING THE PROPHETS IS A WORTHWHILE EXERCISE AS YOU DRAW CLOSER TO THE HEART OF GOD.

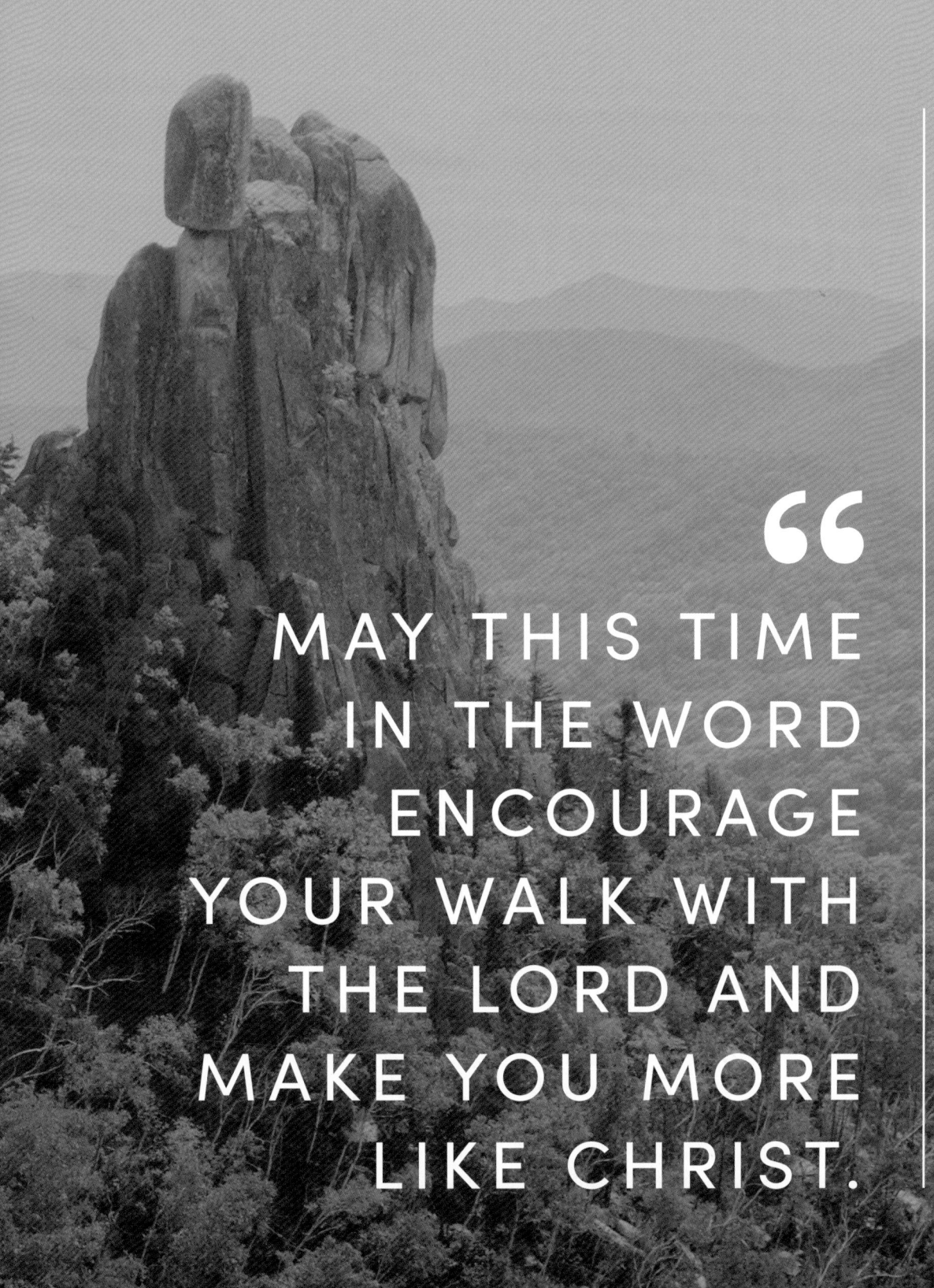

> MAY THIS TIME IN THE WORD ENCOURAGE YOUR WALK WITH THE LORD AND MAKE YOU MORE LIKE CHRIST.

INTRODUCTION TO JOEL

READ JOEL 1–3

There are a handful of books in the Bible that receive heavy foot traffic. Readers are often drawn to the Psalms, Proverbs, the Gospels, or Paul's letters. Each one is wonderful and worth every minute of study, but what about some of those smaller, lesser-known books? You know, those books that require a quick look at the table of contents to remember exactly where to find them—those tiny books like Joel.

The book of Joel is just three short chapters, nestled in the midst of the Old Testament. Found shortly after the Major Prophets and at the beginning of the Minor Prophets, it can be easily skimmed and quickly forgotten in a Bible reading plan. It is not typically a book that comes to mind when choosing the next group Bible study or a passage to walk through in a quiet time. But, though it may be small, Joel has many lessons for the believer both now and for the future.

The message shared in this book is worth taking some time to ponder and study. However, before diving into the book of Joel, it is important to understand four things: the overall message of this book, what we know about Joel as a person and a prophet, the time period in which Joel was written, and the structure and themes of the book. These elements will inform your study as you learn about Joel in the next three weeks.

As for the overall message of Joel, Joel is filled with hard topics and hopeful events. Both are important for the study of this book.

> "WE SHOULD STUDY JOEL FOR THE FUTURE HOPE IT PROVIDES BELIEVERS.

JOEL'S MESSAGE CAN BE TRUSTED BECAUSE
GOD CAN BE TRUSTED.

"

Before we relegate Joel to a dusty shelf with other Minor Prophets that might be difficult to understand, we should study Joel for the future hope it provides believers. God's message spoken through the prophet Joel provides a solemn reminder that we are all sinful and must seek repentance, but it also reminds sinners that their loving and gracious God restores them when they return to Him.

Not much is known about Joel the prophet. The book's opening line states he is the son of Pethuel, and scholars define his name as, "Yahweh is God." No other personal information is given in his prophecy. The other traits known about him are gleaned from the context of his message. He knew the geography and history of Judah and Jerusalem well, implying he was a native. He also understood the inner workings of the temple. While the reader might like to know more about the author, it is important to remember that the true author is God. God gave His words to Joel to share an urgent and important message with the southern kingdom, known as Judah. Joel's message can be trusted because God can be trusted.

Scholars have debated the date Joel was written for many years. As a nation, Israel split into two kingdoms after Solomon's reign. Some believe Joel was written before the northern kingdom fell to Assyria in 722 BC, while some believe it was shortly before Judah, the southern kingdom, fell to Babylon sometime between 587 and 586 BC. Still, others think it was written after some of the Israelites returned from exile. Dating books of the Bible is important for context because it allows us, as readers, to understand the original audience and the cultural activities of the time. What makes Joel unique is that the events of the book can be placed in these different eras and still have the same urgency and application. Therefore, instead of focusing on the time period of the writing, the reader is forced to focus on the message and intent, which will be discussed throughout this study.

Joel is broken into three time periods. In chapter 1, a plague of locusts destroys everything during a prosperous time. In chapter 2, Joel uses the locusts metaphorically to warn the people of a coming army that will destroy them unless they repent. Finally, in chapter 3, Joel shares an eschatological prophecy, which simply means a prophecy concerning the end times.

Though limited in length, Joel covers some significant themes in these chapters. Through the course of this study, themes like the Day of Lord, repentance, mercy, and God's presence will weave together to remind the original audience, Judah, and the present-day audience, us, of God's sovereignty. Whether it was written in the eighth century or the fifth century, Joel's message stands the test of time for readers to learn from the past and prepare for the future.

No matter how difficult it may seem to understand the text, this reminder from 2 Timothy 3:16–17 should spur us on in our study: "All Scripture is inspired by God and is profitable for teaching, for rebuking, for correcting, for training in righteousness, so that the man of God may be complete, equipped for every good work." The study of Joel will help turn our hearts toward our sovereign God, who will complete and equip us in our mission to be more like Jesus. Grab your Bible, and open that table of contents to hunt for Joel one last time. In three weeks, it will hopefully be a place that feels like home and reminds you of the beautiful restoration God provides for His children.

RESPOND

What questions do you have after reading through Joel? Write several of them down. What excites you about studying this book? What intimidates you?

RESPOND

What repeating words and themes do you find as you read Joel?

Day of the LORD
divine imagery
repent
Judgement, destruction
Salvation

As you begin your study of Joel, write out a prayer asking the Lord to give you clarity in the hard places, conviction of your sin, and the perseverance you need to finish well.

Dear God, please send Mary & I your spirit as we embark on this study of Joel together. Speak to us your truths. Help us come to see you more clearly. Help us to be convicted of our sin, and give us a stronger desire to turn to you in repentance.
In Christ's name,
Amen

NOTES

GENERATION TO GENERATION

READ JOEL 1:1–4, EXODUS 10:1–15

If you have ever written a letter, you typically begin with a salutation and some form of greeting. What follows next is possibly some "small talk" and then your purpose for writing. Many of the books in the Bible loosely follow that pattern. Joel, however, keeps things short and to the point. Joel begins by plainly stating that his message is the word of the Lord. Specifically, he writes, "The word of the Lord that came to Joel son of Pethuel" (Joel 1:1). With this brief introduction, Joel does not present himself as special or worthy of notoriety. He reminds his audience this message is divine. It comes from the very heart and mind of God. He simply points to the ultimate author and shares the message.

The definition of a prophet is "a person regarded as an inspired teacher or proclaimer of the will of God." Prophets typically addressed specific people or groups of people. Joel addressed a large group of people in Judah, the southern kingdom. The city of Jerusalem is also mentioned several times in Joel. Jerusalem was the capital of Judah and the home of the temple where many of the people addressed in this book gathered. In these first few verses, Joel directs his comments to specific people. However, Joel also calls the nation as a whole to listen.

The first group of people Joel addresses are the elders. The term "elders" may have referred to the government leaders in the community, the older citizens, or possibly both. In light of Joel's message to Judah, both are logical. Joel tells the elders to "hear,"

"IN HIS GREAT MERCY AND GRACE, GOD DOES NOT LEAVE HIS PEOPLE IN DESPAIR.

WHILE THE LOCUST BRINGS DEVASTATION AND DESPAIR,
JESUS BRINGS RESTORATION AND HEALING.

>

and then he tells all the inhabitants of the land to "listen." This might seem redundant, but the roots of these words actually mean different things. The Hebrew root word for "hear" means "to hear intelligently—often with implication of attention, obedience." And the Hebrew root word for "listen" essentially means "to broaden out one's ear" or, in today's terms, "to cup one's hand behind their ear to better hear." Although different words are used to address the different groups of people, the next verse makes it clear that Joel expected both groups to follow his instructions.

Joel tells the elders and inhabitants of the land to share the forthcoming message with their children, their children's children, and the next generation. In total, he asks them to pass it down through the fourth generation. Passing the word of the Lord down through the generations had been practiced for thousands of years. In Deuteronomy 6, Moses tells the people to love the Lord their God with all their heart, soul, and might, and he instructs them to teach this diligently to their children. Sharing the message of God from generation to generation was how the people learned and remembered God's commands. Joel reminds the elders and inhabitants of Judah that it is their job to pass this on to the next generation. These events must not be forgotten.

The major event Joel refers to is a plague of locusts, which had come and utterly ravaged the land. Joel describes the locusts as devouring, swarming, young, and destroying. This progression shows that nothing was left after the locusts finished. All vegetation and stockpiled supplies were gone. Locusts were dreaded and feared in agrarian cultures. Not only would they destroy what was currently growing, but they so devastated the land that nothing grew in the next season. Everything was stripped from the people, and they had nowhere else to turn but the Lord.

The people of Judah knew firsthand what locusts could do, but they also knew what locusts had done in their history. In Exodus 10, the eighth plague on Egypt was locusts. These locusts were thick and destroyed all that was left of Egypt's vegetation. Egypt had already been ravaged by seven other plagues as Pharaoh's heart was continually hardened against freeing the enslaved Israelites. The history of the ten plagues and Israel's eventual exodus were passed from generation to generation. Joel calls these elders and their children to pass along this current event of locusts as well. These humbling stories were meant to draw the people back to God and remind them of their need and dependence on Him for their very life.

While this first chapter can be disheartening, in His great mercy and grace, God does not leave His people in despair. He does not abandon the people of Judah, nor does He abandon us. His plan has always been to provide a Savior. While the locust brings devastation and despair, Jesus brings restoration and healing. Sin has devoured our lives, but Jesus restores and renews. He abounds in steadfast love and faithfulness. Though a season is hard, He is trustworthy. Hard truths remain for Judah in the book of Joel, but God's abundant grace will abound for them and for us because of Jesus.

Living on this side of the cross enables believers to view these first verses with great hope. On the surface, these verses may lead to despair and agony, which resonate across history. However, we know that all of this ultimately pointed to their need for a Savior, whom God was faithful to provide. The same is true in our own lives. The message of Jesus compels us to share who He is from generation to generation. We do this by fulfilling the mission Jesus left for us: to go and make disciples. Those disciples could be coworkers, your children, or the Bible study group you lead. Listen then go and tell the world about Jesus.

RESPOND

Read Psalm 78:1–8. How might the elders and children in Joel's time have learned from these verses? What lessons can you learn or be reminded of in your current season of life?

- passing down stories about the "glorious deeds of Yahweh"
  - because rebellion & failure to do so ↑ they now are told to pass down stories of destruction (ironic)
- share the goodness of God, tell others how he has worked in your life
- spread news of Jesus to children

RESPOND

Joel tells the elders to "hear" and the inhabitants to "listen" to the message from the Lord, and afterward, to tell generation to generation. How do you share the gospel with the next generation? Pray that those you share Jesus with would come to know Him.

- Currently (for a couple more weeks) Mercy & I are teaching CE to K/1st
- need to do more in this area

Think of a season when the "locusts" devoured and destroyed your life. What did God teach you during that season, and how did Jesus bring hope and restoration?

- that he is the only solution
- by repentance

NOTES

WAIL & MOURN

READ JOEL 1:5–10, NUMBERS 28:1–8

The locusts have devoured everything, and Judah is now a desolate land. Joel has just finished addressing the elders and the inhabitants of the land, imploring them to share this message with the generations as a warning. He now turns to another audience and calls them to respond to this national disaster. But more importantly, they must respond to God, the One they have forsaken.

Joel describes the locusts as a nation invading the land. They were so numerous and so powerful that they devastated everything from the ground to the grapevine to the fig tree. Nothing remained. In a farming culture that had experienced abundance, this loss was felt from king to peasant, from priest to drunkard. No one was exempt from the lessons God had for them.

The best way to describe the drunkards mentioned in Joel 1:5 is to think of them as pleasure-seekers—people who are apathetic to their own moral decay. Joel is addressing a broader audience of Israelites who no longer put God first. Their desire for enjoyment and satisfaction in worldly pleasures drives their loyalty to themselves. God has stripped away the object of their happiness. The locusts destroyed all food, including the grapes of the vine, which supplied the people with wine. Once the wine dried up, everyone, especially the drunkards, would keenly feel the loss, as wine was a large part of the culture and was used for celebrations and enjoyment at meals.

The removal of wine from Judah's culture is one of the reasons Joel calls for the drunkards to wake up. They must weep and wail over

"GOD IS THE ONLY ONE WHO IS DEPENDABLE AND LASTING.

LAY YOUR SIN AT THE CROSS, LEAVE IT THERE, AND
WALK WITH JESUS TO THE THRONE OF THE FATHER.

"

the destruction of their land, but even more so, they must cry out over their indifference to their sin. God has exposed their vice and eliminated it. They have nowhere else to turn but to God. Over and over, the words "weep," "wail," "mourn," and "grieve" are used to call the people to action. The people are to grieve like a young bride who loses her husband, mourn like a priest who can no longer bring offerings to the Lord, and grieve like the land that is destroyed. God has stripped away the worldly things that brought Judah comfort. He desires for His people's complete dependence on Him. Stripping these things away is for Judah's good so that they will trust in God alone and not the things of this world, as God is the only One who is dependable and lasting.

Though God is working to remove strongholds from the people of Judah, the knowledge that God cannot be in the presence of sin is nothing new to the Israelites. Throughout Exodus, Leviticus, and Numbers, God gives detailed instructions to Moses and the priests for how to atone for the sin of the nation so that people can be made right with God. God is holy, set apart, and blameless. He is just and must punish sin. He is righteous, and His entire being is morally perfect. For man to stand before God requires a sacrifice. The priests in Joel's time were still performing these offerings on behalf of the people. However, they were being performed out of tradition—not repentance. Now, God has deprived them of the very items they need for forgiveness: the sacrifice. Eventually, the consequences God instills will bring His people back into a right relationship with Him, where they will truly thrive. But for now, in Joel 1, the people must grieve because their worship of God is compromised.

Sin will always cause compromise. It will make us cold and callous toward our Creator. Sin will convince us that our need for pleasure and happiness is more important than a relationship with the God of the universe. Sin makes a lot of promises but never keeps them. It prevents us from a relationship with God because He cannot be in the presence of sin. His holiness requires a sacrificial payment.

For thousands of years, the priests would sacrifice before the Lord. The offerings were a pleasing aroma to Him and temporarily quenched His wrath. Thankfully, God had a plan for a sacrifice who would forever atone for man's sins. God, in His great love and wisdom, sent Jesus to be the ultimate and final sacrifice. First Peter 3:18 tells us, "For

Christ also suffered for sins once for all, the righteous for the unrighteous, that he might bring you to God. He was put to death in the flesh but made alive by the Spirit." The blood of the spotless Lamb, Jesus, brings you to God. You are now a pleasing aroma to the Lord. You can stand before Him covered by the blood of Jesus, who bore God's wrath on your behalf.

What a gift and blessing that we can rejoice in salvation through Jesus! But we have to be vigilant in our battle against sin. Just like the people of Judah, apathy in our relationship with God easily creeps in. We take the good things God gives us, and we pervert them or obsess over them, thus placing them on the throne of our lives. We must repent, seek forgiveness, and press on toward sanctification, our journey to be more like Christ. Do you grieve over your sin? Is it your desire to live a life that is a pleasing aroma to the Lord? Do not allow the locusts of life to come in and devastate in order to draw you back to God. Just as Joel says in verse 5, "Wake up!" Lay your sin at the cross, leave it there, and walk with Jesus to the throne of the Father. It is there that you will flourish and have no need for mourning.

RESPOND

Judah was called to wail, weep, and mourn over their sin. What sin do you need to confess and mourn?

lust
quick-temperedness
self-control
covetousness
idolatry

RESPOND

According to Titus 2:11–15, how can you fight against the temptation to continue in your sin?

- Study the grace of God
- Know the grace of God
- Read Scripture & Pray over it
- eagerly wait the parousia
- Sit under the preaching of the Word
- Seek counsel for biblical guidance & exhortation & rebuke
- take hold of faith
- pray for more faith

Read Psalm 51. This is the psalm David wrote after the prophet Nathan called him to repent for his adulterous sin with Bathsheba (2 Samuel 11–12). Write your own prayer of repentance, and praise God for His grace and forgiveness.

LORD, have mercy on me. Blot out my transgressions. Make me white as snow. Forgive me, Lord, for I have sinned against you. All my life, without you, I am sin. Without you, I have no hope. Lord, let the hope of eternal salvation take deep roots in my soul. Grant me transforming grace. Renew my heart, sanctify it more and more. Change my desires. Give me a greater desire to serve you, a stronger appetite for your Word and obedience to it. I praise you, Lord, for sending Jesus because without him, I was dead forever. Thank you, thank you, thank you.

In his name, I come to you,

Amen

NOTES

Sin has devastating consequences.
There is no running from these consequences.
There is no "secret sin." God sees all.
Sin destroys your relationship w/ the Lord.

FEAST OR FAMINE

READ JOEL 1:11–12, EXODUS 23:10–16, JOHN 15:1–8

Joel has just finished sharing a hard message of wailing and mourning with the pleasure-seekers and priests who live in the city. It would seem some sort of hopeful message is around the corner. Hope will come, but not just yet. Joel's message now shifts to the very people who toil the land and would feel the loss of the harvest most keenly. They are not spared from the Lord's discipline.

The farmers outside the city are not exempt from wailing and mourning this national disaster. They felt this devastation twofold. Not only was there no harvest to enjoy, but all the hours they labored in the sun were also wasted. God calls them to be ashamed of the sin that wreaked such havoc on their livelihood. The lack of harvest also affected their ability to bring offerings to the temple and celebrate festival seasons.

Exodus 23:10–16 gives a glimpse into the importance of the land and the harvest. The harvest was meant to promote Sabbath rest, care for the poor, rest the land, and bring the firstfruits as a sacrifice to the Lord. Festivals were regular celebrations of God's faithfulness to His people. Often called "feasts," each festival was a time of great joy and thanksgiving in worship to God. They would last for several days or even a week. The loss of the harvest prevented the farmers from bringing the firstfruits as an offering and experiencing the joy of a productive season. God desired for the work of their hands to point to His goodness and provision.

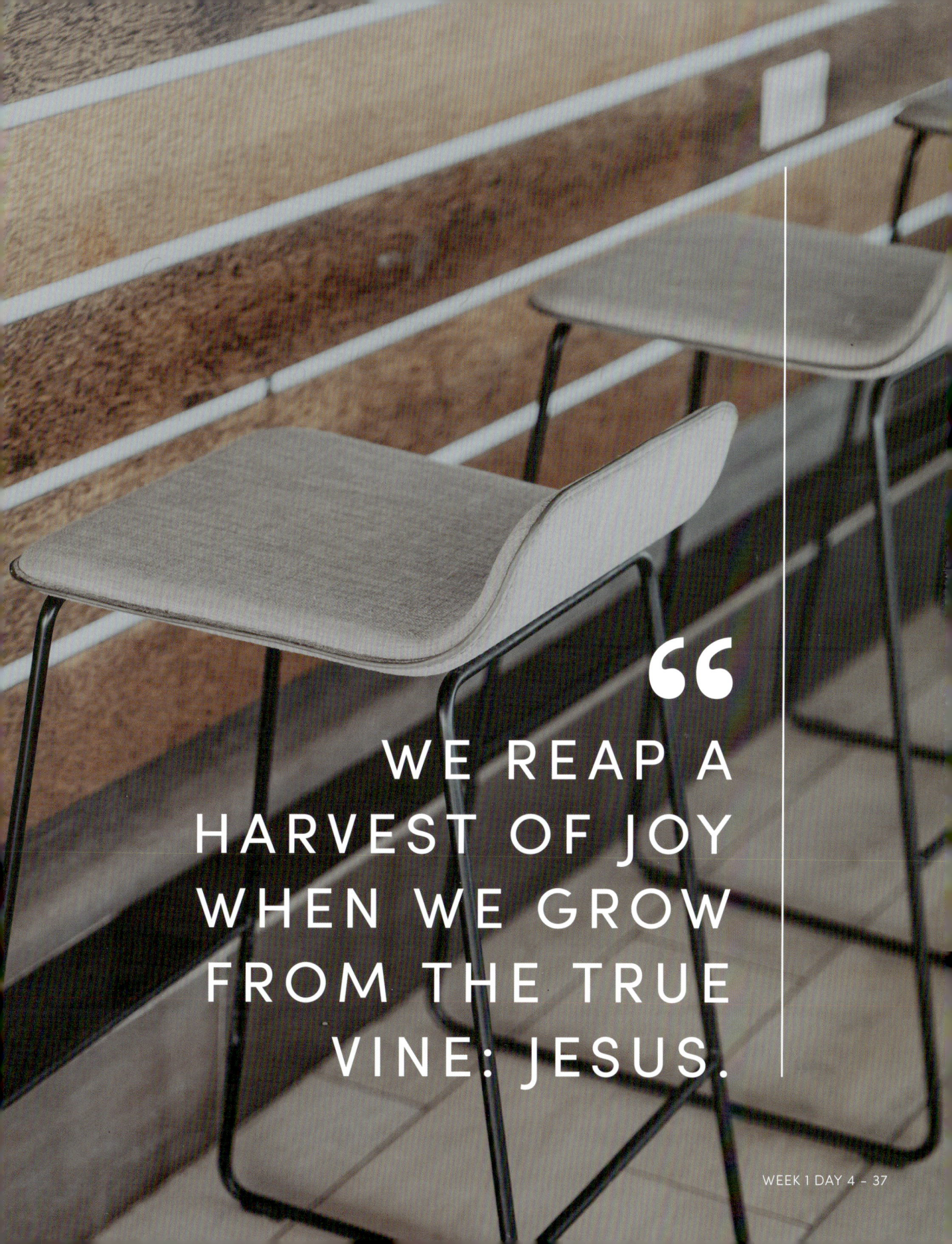

LET THE GARDENER PRUNE AND CULTIVATE YOU TO BE
A MAGNIFICENT DISPLAY OF HIS HANDIWORK.

"

They were to find joy in the spiritual and physical blessings gifted by God. What was meant to be a season of celebration now brought shame and mourning.

To add insult to injury, Joel uses the words "dried up" as he imparts his message. This implies that not only did the locusts come and destroy the land, but a drought fell upon the nation as well. The crops were destroyed, as were the grapevine, the fig trees, and all the trees of the orchard. Throughout the Old Testament, the grapevine and fig tree were symbols of the blessing of God's relationship with His chosen people, Israel. Israel was the vine God planted, but instead of yielding good grapes, Israel became degenerate (Jeremiah 2:21). The people turned their backs on God and sought to produce a harvest in their own strength. Without the work of the true Gardener, the land dried up, and all human joy was lost (Joel 1:12).

It is easy to imagine that the farmers felt hopeless and joyless. Their livelihood was gone, and they had nothing to sacrifice at the festivals. Yet God is using this devastation to call them back to a right relationship with Him, just as He did with the pleasure-seekers and the priests in Joel 1:5–9. Despite their hopelessness, with trust in God, there is always hope, both for the Israelite in Joel's time and for the believer in the twenty-first century. The coming Messiah was the hope of Israel then, and the already-come Messiah, Jesus, is our hope today. A relationship with Jesus is the only place we find joy. Reconciliation to God through Jesus's death, burial, and resurrection is the fertile ground where joy grows.

The Apostle John quotes Jesus in John 15:1, 5, when He says, "I am the true vine, and my Father is the gardener. . . . I am the vine; you are the branches. The one who remains in me and I in him produces much fruit, because you can do nothing without me." We reap a harvest of joy when we grow from the true Vine: Jesus. That does not mean there will never be locusts and famine in our lives. Hard times will come, but through Jesus, we are promised to produce much fruit. When we toil the soil of our lives in our own power, the meager amount of fruit produced will pale in comparison to what God can produce through us. You can find joy in your Savior because you are growing in the Gardener's time. He will give you fruit that lasts, fruit that will be joyfully returned as a sacrifice.

Joy can often seem elusive in a world filled with sin. It certainly was for those in Joel's time after such devastation. But, as John 15 reminds us, joy is rooted in our relationship with God through Jesus. Apart from Him, human joy is fleeting and simply an emotion we seek in earthly pleasures. If our relationship with the Lord is not right and healthy, true joy will only ever be an exercise in futility and emptiness. We must learn from the mistakes of those who came before us. Joel's message to the farmers serves as a reminder for us today: be rooted in Christ. The Bible is where we find all we need to live a life that *sufficiency* seeks to serve the Lord through the toil of our hands and the sacrifice of our life. Let the Gardener prune and cultivate you to be a magnificent display of His handiwork.

RESPOND

In what ways are you seeking to produce a harvest of faith in your own strength? *good or bad?*

RESPOND

What are some examples from your life where you have seen sin dry up your joy and whither your relationship with the Lord? What steps must you take for the Lord to reap a harvest again?

- Sexual immorality, repent, continual repentance
  ↳ it's not a true repentance if I keep "struggling" w/ failures

Lord, in my future ministry & in it now, please be the light. Let not others look at me and see me for my old self, but let my new identity in Christ be ever shining. If I rely on my own strength for my ministry, it will be fruitless; Lord, please go before me. Please be with me constantly. Please guide me. Let "my" ministry be the ministry that you give me. Prepare me in my final year or so of seminary for being above-reproach so that I may glorify you through ordained ministry. In Christ's name, Amen.

Read Psalm 1. How could the people of Judah have learned from this passage? How does this passage serve as both a warning and encouragement to you?

- They chose the path of the wicked, they did not walk in the law of the LORD; thus, they withered & did not yield any more fruit.

NOTES

See Jer. 14 for more info on drought/famine during exile.

THE DAY OF THE LORD IS NEAR

READ JOEL 1:13–20

Yesterday's reading closed with the people of Judah, from every walk of life, wailing and mourning the loss of their economy to the locusts, just as Joel told them to. The message does not end with wailing and mourning, though. Those emotional responses were easily provoked out of desperation. But emotions do not require further action on the people's behalf. They can wail and then continue on in their sinful posture toward God, hopeful He will bless them again. It does not truly cost them anything to stay in the same patterns of life. But, through Joel, God calls them to action, and He has the priests lead the nation in lament. If the people do not truly repent from their transgression, they will experience the weight of the Lord's wrath and devastation, and it will pale in comparison to locusts.

Today, Joel turns his message back to the priests of the land. Their job was to be the religious leaders for the people and sacrifice on their behalf. The desolation of all crops had stopped the sacrifices in the temple. The priests and the people should not lament the loss of their economic success but instead mourn the loss of their ability to worship God. Joel calls the priests to begin their repentance by dressing in sackcloth. Made of goat or stiff camel hair, the Israelites often wore sackcloths in times of mourning (Genesis 37:34). Sackcloths were uncomfortable and would have reminded the priests of the emotional anguish and discomfort their sin should cause.

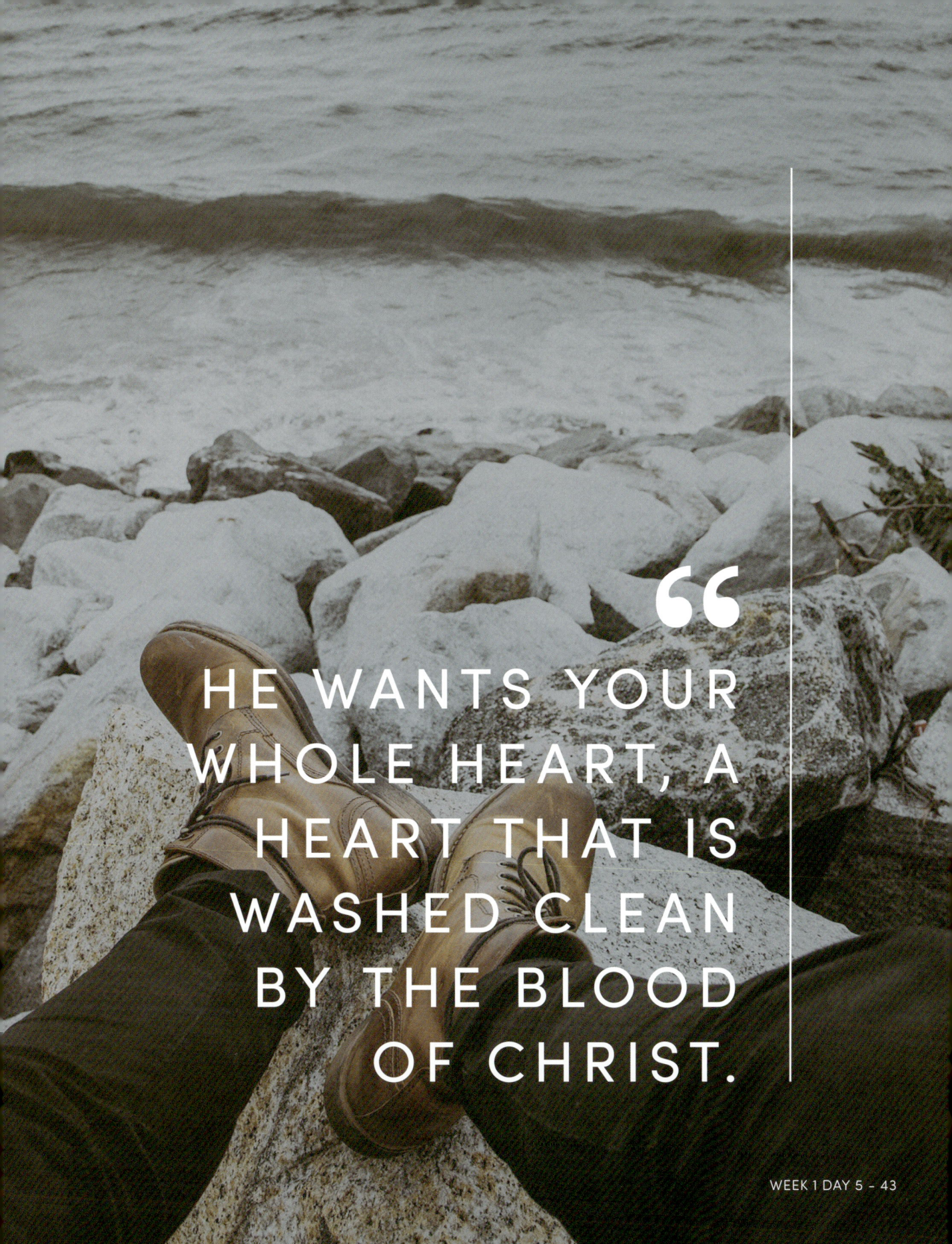

GREET THE DAY OF THE LORD WITH JOY BECAUSE YOU
TRUST IN CHRIST.

"

As spiritual leaders, God called the priests to lead the people in a national fast. This was a fast from all food for a specified amount of time. The priests were to gather all the inhabitants of the land—including the elders of the land, the pleasure-seekers, and the farmers. All inhabitants were to come to the temple, fast, and cry out to the Lord. This was a call to action. The people had a choice to make: either repent and seek the Lord's restoration or experience the Day of the Lord—the day when God's wrath would be poured out in judgment. The Day of the Lord would be far more fearsome than their current circumstances. The physical discomfort of sackcloth and fasting should remind them of their spiritual discomfort—a discomfort that would increase if they did not return to the Lord.

In case the people wondered how it could ever get worse, Joel quickly reminds them of the devastation around them. The obvious state of their condition and the possibility of it being increased ten-fold on the Day of the Lord should cause the people to lament. The people are reminded that their sin also affects the very animals that they own to work the land. These cattle, sheep, and goats suffer punishment and lament because there is nothing to eat and nowhere to house them. Joel seems to be asking the people, *If the animals cry out, why do we not?* Judah groans under the weight of their rebellion. And their repentance begins at the temple, crying out and fasting before the Lord.

After explaining the state of society, Joel turns in prayer to the Lord. He says, "I call to you, Lord" (Joel 1:19). Joel lets the people know they must repent personally, but he also intercedes on their behalf. They must not forget that even the animals, land, and rivers cry out to the God of all creation. Their souls must long for God as the deer longs for the water (Psalm 42:1). Only in His presence would they be satisfied, forgiven, and redeemed. If they choose to continue in sin, the future is bleak and filled with anguish as the Lord pours out His wrath on this rebellious nation.

The Day of the Lord is a fearsome thing but not for those who are in Christ. God desires that all come to repentance and not perish (2 Peter 3:9). That is why He sent His Son to be the ultimate sacrifice. No longer must we come before God in sackcloth and mourn at the temple. We can lay our sin at the foot of the cross where Jesus defeated sin and death once and for all. Jesus even lamented on our behalf while on the cross.

In Luke 23:34, He said, "Father, forgive them, because they do not know what they are doing." We often think this comment only applies to the people who put Him on the cross, but it also applies to us. We are quick to forget that our sin made us executioners as well. But lament turned to joy on that resurrection Sunday, and we now have access to the Father. We can trust that God forgives our sins, and we will not experience the pain and agony of the Day of the Lord.

While we await the day of the Lord's return, there is still work to do. God calls us to action for our sin, just as Joel called Judah on God's behalf. In our society driven by self-fulfillment, we often either do not repent at all, or we say just enough to get by. God desires more, and He is not fooled by fake apologies or deals made to get out of trouble. He wants your whole heart, a heart that is washed clean by the blood of Christ—a heart that desires to live life for Him and proclaim Jesus to others. The time has come to mourn and lament our sin before our Holy God—to pray for forgiveness and the strength to never return to that sinful place, to feel the weight of sin that put Jesus on that cross. It is when we return to a right relationship with God that we will lay aside the sin that ensnares and run the race that lies before us (Hebrews 12:1). Greet the Day of the Lord with joy because you trust in Christ.

RESPOND

Have you ever fasted from food or drink or something else in your life? If so, how did it deepen your relationship with God? If you have not fasted before, what concerns you about the process? Write a prayer asking God to help you know how to begin this act of worship to Him.

RESPOND

In addition to their mourning, Joel calls the priests and the people to action. What action steps do you need to take to truly repent from sin in your life?

What sin has Jesus given you victory over? Read Psalm 30, and celebrate His faithfulness to turn lament into dancing.

NOTES

SCRIPTURE MEMORY

I AM THE TRUE VINE, AND MY FATHER IS THE GARDENER. . . . I AM THE VINE; YOU ARE THE BRANCHES. THE ONE WHO REMAINS IN ME AND I IN HIM PRODUCES MUCH FRUIT, BECAUSE YOU CAN DO NOTHING WITHOUT ME.

JOHN 15:1, 5

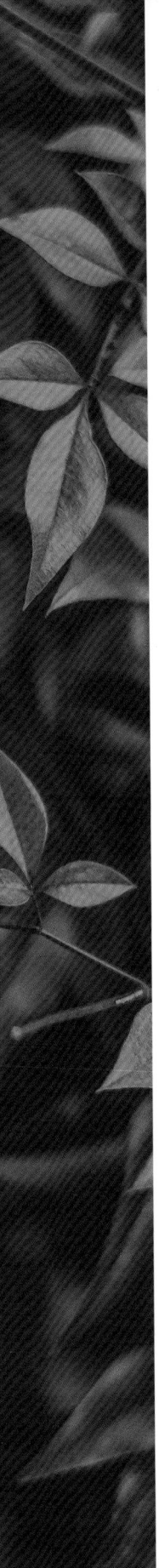

Practice memorizing this week's Scripture by writing it out below.

WEEK ONE REFLECTION

REVIEW JOEL 1

01

Paraphrase the passage from this week.

02

What did you observe from this week's text about God and His character?

03

What does this week's passage reveal about the condition of mankind and yourself?

---- 04

How does this passage point to the gospel?

---- 05

How should you respond to this passage? What specific action steps can you take this week to apply this passage?

---- 06

Write a prayer in response to your study of God's Word. Adore God for who He is, confess sins that He revealed in your own life, ask Him to empower you to walk in obedience, and pray for anyone who comes to mind as you study.

THE DAY OF THE LORD IS COMING

READ JOEL 2:1–11, AMOS 5:18–20, MATTHEW 24:29–31, 36–44

The people of Judah have gathered at the temple to cry out to the Lord, lament, and fast over their sin. They see the utter destruction around them and await the continuation of Joel's message from the Lord. They likely felt exhausted, defeated, and sorrowful from the devastation of their livelihood. It is in this humbled state that Joel's message takes a turn. He begins a narration of future events, pointing to the fact that the locusts were only a precursor to impending judgment if the people did not turn back to the Lord. Joel uses the picture of the invading locusts in chapter 1 as an analogy for an invading army on the Day of the Lord. This army will appear like the dawn, swarming the land and devouring it (Joel 2:2–5). They will stay their course and infiltrate the city (Joel 2:6–9), and Judah will feel the dread of the Lord of Armies (Joel 2:10–11).

In ancient Jerusalem, the ram's horn was used to sound the alarm and warn the people of impending danger and invasion. Zion, known as the throne of the Lord, would have implied the temple mount where the presence of the Lord dwelt. Joel prophesies about the Day of the Lord, telling the people that the sounding of the horn from the temple will cause great fear, dread, and trembling among the people at the arrival of a great army. Just as the dawn spreads across the land, touching everything in its path, this army will leave a wasteland. Like the locusts, the army will devour with great discipline in the same way as galloping

> **JUST AS FIRE ROARS AND CONSUMES EVERYTHING IN ITS PATH, NO ONE WILL ESCAPE THE DAY OF THE LORD.**

> **FOR THOSE WHO FOLLOW CHRIST, THE TRUMPET WILL SOUND, AND WE WILL BE WITH HIM FOR ETERNITY.**

war horses and chariots deployed for war. Just as fire roars and consumes everything in its path, no one will escape the Day of the Lord.

Such impending doom and destruction will cause faces to pale and the people to writhe in horror. The well-trained army will stay its course until the job is complete. They will move as one and accomplish the purpose of their leader: the Lord. The city walls will not keep them out, and they will enter through windows to plunder and destroy. Joel wants the people to understand that the locust invasion is nothing compared to the judgment to come. No one can get away from it, and everyone must pay for their rebellion against God.

The people can trust that this army will succeed because it is led by the sovereign God. God alone controls the land and the sky, which quakes with His coming. He commands the sun, moon, and stars to cease their shining in this impending doom. He is the Lord of Armies exalted by His justice, and He demonstrates His holiness through His righteousness (Isaiah 5:16).

Joel ends this section by reminding the people, if they have not figured it out yet, that the Day of the Lord is terrible and dreadful, and none can endure it. The prophet Amos also spoke of the Day of Lord, further emphasizing, "What will the day of the Lord be for you? It will be darkness and not light. It will be like a man who flees from a lion only to have a bear confront him. He goes home and rests his hand against the wall only to have a snake bite him" (Amos 5:18–19).

Yet again, there seems to be no hope for the people of Judah. In the following verses and chapters, God will tell His children what they can do to stay His wrath. But sadly, over time, their hearts continued in rebellion, and God eventually sent an army to destroy them. Since we do not know the exact dating of Joel, this could be the conquering Assyrian or Babylonian armies. Both were fearsome and like no army that had walked the earth. Whichever army it was, the implication for Judah—and for us—is to take seriously the command God makes to return to Him and repent from our sinful ways.

Thankfully, the message does not end here, but it is important to stop and think about the implications of such a day. Even in the twenty-first century, we await the coming of the Day of the Lord. Judah has already experienced a reckoning for her rebellion, but all of mankind awaits the final judgment now. In His mercy, grace, and love, God did not abandon us. He sent Jesus to pay the price for our sin. As He promised in the gospels, He will return, though no one knows the day or the hour (Matthew 24:36–44). His return will bring joy for those who know Him and dread for those who do not. His army of angels will be like no army ever seen. For those who follow Christ, the trumpet will sound, and we will be with Him for eternity. For those who do not follow Him, great darkness, weeping, and turmoil await (Matthew 24:29–31).

Are you ready? When Christ returns, will you be part of the elect He brings to the new heaven and new earth, or will hopelessness and separation from God be your destination? If we have learned anything from Joel thus far, it is that we serve a holy and righteous God who desires repentant hearts and complete worship. He wants us to lament our sin, find forgiveness in Christ, and walk in His ways as we share the message of Jesus with a lost world. Do not be surprised by Christ's return. Be ready for the Day of the Lord.

RESPOND

Have you sought forgiveness from Jesus and given your life to Him? If yes, take a moment to praise Him for your salvation and the hope you have for the future. If not, take some time to seek Jesus. Ask Him to give you the desire to seek forgiveness and serve Him with your life.

RESPOND

Second Peter 3:13–14 says, "But based on his promise, we wait for new heavens and a new earth, where righteousness dwells. Therefore, dear friends, while you wait for these things, make every effort to be found without spot or blemish in his sight, at peace." What can you do to be found without spot or blemish as you wait for the Lord?

Read Psalm 84. Do you long for the courts of the Lord? What do you look forward to most one day when you will dwell in the house of the Lord?

NOTES

RETURN TO THE LORD

READ JOEL 2:12–17, PSALM 86

WEEK 02 / DAY 02

Joel's message to the people of Judah has been hard thus far. They have been through the devastation of the locust plague and been warned about the terrible, dreadful Day of the Lord. God has their attention, and He will now share His deep concern for His people and His desire that they turn back to Him. The verses in this passage are broken into two major sections. First, God's character will be on full display. Next, Judah must take practical steps to repent and take action.

God's immediate message to Judah is that they should turn to Him with all their heart. They are not just to tear their clothes symbolically; they are to tear their very hearts. The people would understand this language from Deuteronomy 30:6 when Moses told the Israelites, "The Lord your God will circumcise your heart and the hearts of your descendants, and you will love him with all your heart and all your soul so that you will live." The act of tearing or circumcising their hearts showed total devotion to God. By returning to Him and giving Him the true worship He is due, they could live.

The people are then reminded of God's very nature. God is gracious, compassionate, slow to anger, and abounding in faithful love. These attributes should not come as a surprise to the nation—they had been spoken many times to Israel in their history. God first spoke these words about Himself in Exodus 34:6. Moses, while leading the people through the wilderness, had gone back

> ## GOD IS GRACIOUS, COMPASSIONATE, SLOW TO ANGER, AND ABOUNDING IN FAITHFUL LOVE.

> ## GOD NEVER CHANGES. HIS CHARACTER REMAINS THE SAME
> ### FROM GENERATION TO GENERATION.

up Mount Sinai to receive the Ten Commandments for a second time. As the Lord passed in front of Moses in a cloud, He declared these very attributes about Himself. It is because God is gracious, compassionate, slow to anger, and faithful that He relents by forgiving iniquity, rebellion, and sin for a thousand generations. Their ancestors had to be reminded of these truths, and now, Judah is reminded as well. Their sins were great, but God's mercy is greater. God never changes. His character remains the same from generation to generation.

In Joel 2:14, God says of Himself, "Who knows? He may turn and relent and leave a blessing behind him." "Who knows?" does not mean God is unsure or undecided. "Who knows?" displays God's sovereignty. This rhetorical question shows He knows the heart of the people, and He knows whether they will turn back or not. Turning back to God would cause Him to relent, and in essence, forgive them for their rebellion. If they do return, God would provide what they need for grain and drink offerings once again. These offerings should be given with a right and repentant heart in true worship and not done in ritual only.

The next section, Joel 2:15–17, calls the people to action. In light of God's character and the mandate He has given, Judah is given four commands. The first command is to blow the ram's horn. Unlike Joel 2:1, when the horn is blown to announce an invading army, this horn is blown to gather the people to repent. Next, a sacred fast is announced, followed by the proclamation of a solemn assembly. This was not a time of joy or feasting. Sin should be lamented, never celebrated. Lastly, all the people are to gather and assemble. This refers back to Joel 1:14 but goes a step further and states that even the babies and the newlyweds must attend. In Israelite culture, newborns and their mothers as well as newlyweds were exempt from feasts and temple gatherings. That privilege was revoked in this solemn hour. Everyone was called to repent as a nation. The priests, as the spiritual leaders, would lead the people in the prayer of repentance. God's relenting would keep the nation from scorn and ridicule, and all nations would remember the God of the Israelites because He never left them.

The wrath of God toward Judah was satiated for a time. However, they eventually turned back to their sinful ways, and God brought judgment through the destruction of the temple and exile of the nation. He always planned to save a small group of His children, a remnant, through which the future Messiah would come. When God stated who He is in Exodus 34:6 and Joel 2:13, Jesus was sitting by His side, waiting for the Father to send Him to be the ultimate physical display of those attributes. Jesus walked the earth for thirty-three years and perfectly exhibited grace, compassion, love, and faithfulness. Through His sacrificial death and resurrection, Jesus provides the way for all people to return to the Father and for the Father's wrath to relent.

Over and over in Scripture, these attributes are repeated by God, the prophets, and the apostles. Psalm 86 is a clear picture of lament, petition, and praise to God. The author of the psalm, David, knew God was who He said He was. No matter the circumstances affecting his life, he could trust God was gracious, compassionate, loving, faithful, and slow to anger. As we face trials in life, when the locusts devour and destroy, our first thought should always be to remember who God is and turn back to Him in true devotion and worship. When we willfully sin, He is gracious and slow to anger. When we desire a way back to Him, He is compassionate and provides the way through Jesus. When we seek Him with our whole heart, He is abounding in faithful love. Praise His name, for He is great and does wondrous things (Psalm 86:10)!

RESPOND

God called the Israelites to action to repent of their sin. What action do you need to take to turn back to God in true devotion and worship?

RESPOND

Write out each of the attributes listed in Joel 2:13. What do they mean, and how do they remind you to worship God with a right heart?

Read David's prayer in Psalm 86, and write out your own prayer to God below.

NOTES

THE LORD IS MERCIFUL

READ JOEL 2:18–24, PSALM 126

As Joel's message unfolds, God continually calls the people to respond in lament and repentance. The message now shifts, and God responds to His people. In Joel 2:14, God hints at the possibility of restoration if the people follow His commands. Now that the people have called out to Him in genuine repentance, restoration is a reality. The prayers uttered by the priests as they led the people were heard, and God is ready to relent and pour out His blessings on His people.

The Lord's message begins by stating He became jealous for His land and His people. This attribute of jealousy is not the human definition of jealousy—an angry desire to have what belongs to other people. Righteous jealousy is simply God desiring the praise and affection He rightly deserves. He is saving His people for the sake of His glory. In response to Judah's repentance, God will now bring relief and blessings. He will show compassion, as Psalm 103:13 states, "As a father has compassion on his children, so the Lord has compassion on those who fear him."

God gives four promises to the people in His response to the people's repentance. All four show His mercy as He holds back His wrath. This will be an era when both their physical and spiritual needs will be met. First, He promises to provide for their needs. All that was lost will be restored. He will send grain, new wine, and fresh oil. The harvest will be plentiful again. Second, He promises that they will no longer be a disgrace to the nations

> ## OUR HEARTS NOW OVERFLOW
> # WITH THE PRESENCE OF OUR SAVIOR.

around them (Joel 2:19). Once again, God will be their God, and they will be His people. For His glory alone, the covenant promises were kept.

Next, God promises to remove the foreign invader (Joel 2:20). The army that was to come from the north to destroy will be turned back, thrown into the sea, and banished to a desolate land. The same words used to describe the land of Judah after the plague of locusts will be used against the invading army. God is the Lord of Armies and has control over every nation. He dictates when invasions occur and who sits on the throne of each nation (Psalm 22:28). The Lord delivers Judah from their enemy.

Lastly, the promise of no more fear and great rejoicing will come to the nation. Here, four subgroups are addressed. The land can rejoice and be glad because it will now produce vegetation and a harvest once again. The animals do not have to be afraid because once again they will have green pastures in which to graze. The fig tree, the vine, and all the fruit trees destroyed by the locusts will yield their riches again. The children of Zion can rejoice and be glad because the Lord showers them with autumn and spring rains. This rain represents the physical blessing for the land and the spiritual blessings of mercy, love, deliverance, and joy. The people will come back from the fields with shouts of joy, carrying their sheaves (Psalm 126:6).

God has relented and shown His great mercy toward His people. We are the recipients of this great mercy, as well, through Jesus Christ. Just like Judah, we are prone to rebellion and idols. Simply put, we are prone to sin. The only way to stay God's wrath and cause Him to relent from judgment toward us is to put our hope and faith in Jesus. The Apostle Paul explains this in 1 Corinthians 5:21 when he writes, "He made the one who did not know sin to be sin for us, so that in him we might become the righteousness of God." Jesus was the perfect sacrifice and took our sin upon Himself so that we could have a relationship with God again. When we bring our sin to Jesus and lament over our rebellion to God, He cleanses us, hears our prayers, and God, in His mercy, relents His wrath. Jesus bore the wrath we deserve. Through Him, we have hope for eternity and experience mercy to the fullest.

In Christ, God now rains down His blessings on us. While these blessings can be physical, far greater are the spiritual blessings of joy, hope, peace, love, and eternal life, to name a few. Though the locusts of sin steal everything from us, through Jesus, we experience restoration and the mercy of God. Our hearts now overflow with the presence of our Savior. We are called to show mercy to others as we emulate Christ. Christ showed mercy in every aspect of His ministry, from healing the sick to calling out the sin of the religious leaders. Mercy marks us as Christ-followers in a world that willingly casts others aside for the smallest offense. Mercy should color how we speak and the actions we take. We are alive in Christ Jesus because of the rich mercy of God (Ephesians 2:4–5). Let us be a people known for our mercy as our lives point back to our merciful God.

RESPOND

Describe a season when God has brought discipline into your life. Did you repent and call on Him to relent? How was He merciful toward you to bring joy to your life again (Psalm 126)?

RESPOND

First Peter 1:3 says, "Blessed be the God and Father of our Lord Jesus Christ. Because of his great mercy he has given us new birth into a living hope through the resurrection of Jesus Christ from the dead." Write a prayer, thanking God for His great mercy and the gift of Jesus.

Jesus was the ultimate example of mercy in His ministry, death, and resurrection. As you follow Him, how can you show mercy in all aspects of your life?

NOTES

THE LORD RESTORES

READ JOEL 2:25–27, EZEKIEL 37:15–28

The Lord has rained down His mercy on the people of Judah after their wholehearted repentance. This rain has been both physical and spiritual as the people once again experienced a harvest and the blessings of God. God's mercy is great, but the restoration He brings will be greater. His abundant grace will bring the people satisfaction, inspire obedience, and spark worship. Restoration will come in the immediate, but Joel's message will speak to restoration in the future as well.

After all the blessings He has rained down on the people, God now promises that He will repay the people for the years the locusts destroyed and the devastation of the great army. God does not just use the single term "locusts" in Joel 2:25. Rather, He repeats each type of locust that was mentioned in Joel 1:4 when the infestation began. God is in the details. He knows exactly what each locust did and how they affected each person. The disaster was great, but God's restoration is greater.

The promise to be satisfied and hungry no more brings restoration to empty stomachs and desperate hearts. The locusts had their time to eat and devour. God has now provided a feast for the people through a bountiful harvest and His bountiful grace. Their stomachs would be full, but more importantly, their hearts would sing the praises of the name of the Lord. He has dealt wondrously with His children, and they now will cry, "Lord, our Lord, how magnificent is your name throughout the earth" (Psalm 8:9)!

> "GOD HAS PERSISTENTLY SOUGHT A RELATIONSHIP WITH HIS CHILDREN FROM THE MOMENT HE CREATED THEM.

WALK IN VICTORY
BECAUSE THE LORD YOUR GOD HAS DEALT WONDROUSLY WITH YOU.

"

The last verse in this section reminds the nation of God's presence in their lives. God has persistently sought a relationship with His children from the moment He created them. The desire to abide with His image-bearers did not die when Adam and Eve sinned. God put into motion the plan of redemption and restoration in which He will one day dwell with His people eternally. Despite sin and rebellion, God's plan of restoration began the moment He promised Eve her seed would crush the head of the serpent (Genesis 3:15). The Messiah would one day come and destroy Satan and sin forever.

As history awaited that time, God's presence was still at work in the world and seeking a relationship with His children. He called Abraham out of his country to be the father of God's chosen people (Genesis 12:1–9). He called Moses from the burning bush and sent him to Egypt to free His people from bondage (Exodus 3). In a pillar of cloud and fire, God led those same people through the wilderness to the long-awaited Promised Land (Numbers 9:15–23). And in Ezekiel 37:15–28, God spoke to the prophet Ezekiel and told him that one day His sanctuary would be among Israel forever. The separated kingdoms would once again be one, and the long-awaited Messiah would sit on the throne of David forever. Those who call Jesus "Lord" will dwell in His presence: "My dwelling place will be with them; I will be their God, and they will be my people" (Ezekiel 37:27). Restoration is found in the everlasting presence of our Creator God.

God also reminds the people twice that they will never again be put to shame (Joel 2:26–27). The shame Israel felt among other nations was palpable. They served an almighty God, yet they would be defeated, exiled, and disciplined. God promises them that while that may be true for a short while, it will not last for eternity. There is no other God like Him, and He would provide ultimate victory through the long-awaited Messiah. Shame will cease to exist, and God will make all things new.

Just like the people of Judah, we are promised restoration. Through the shed blood of Jesus, salvation is freely given to all people. Scripture tells us, "Everyone who believes on him will not be put to shame, since there is no distinction between Jew and Greek, because the same Lord of all richly blesses all who call on him. For everyone who calls on the name of the Lord will be saved" (Romans 10:11–13).

If you are still struggling with shame over sin you have repented from, remember that Jesus conquered your sin and shame on the cross. Whatever your sin struggle or the past sin that brings you shame, take it to Jesus, and leave it there. He will not turn you away. He will forgive you and wrap you in His loving arms. Walk in victory because the Lord your God has dealt wondrously with you (Joel 2:26). The locusts are gone, and you have been restored to a right relationship with the Father!

RESPOND

Just as Judah repented of their sin and returned to the Lord, is there any unconfessed sin in your life that you need to repent from? Do not hide it any longer, but bring it to the Lord, asking Him for the forgiveness and grace freely given through Jesus.

RESPOND

Over what previously confessed sin does Satan continually make you feel shame? Read Psalm 103:11–13. How can these verses help you leave that shame at the cross and move forward in victory and restoration?

Write a prayer thanking the Lord for His plan of restoration. Thank Him for Jesus and salvation. Thank Him for the future promise that we will dwell in His presence forever.

NOTES

THE PROMISE OF THE SPIRIT

READ JOEL 2:28–32, ACTS 2:1–36

WEEK 02 / DAY 05

God has rained down physical blessings on Judah and restored what the locusts destroyed. His message will now turn to the spiritual blessings He will pour out, not only on Israel but on all who seek Him. God continues His direct address to the people through His prophet, Joel. It is in these verses that we will see a shift to future blessings.

All previous verses in Joel represented a near-fulfillment of prophecy. This means the events Joel shared with the people happened during Joel's lifetime. In these next five verses, it is important to understand that God shifts to sharing events that would have a future fulfillment centuries later in the church age, followed by an eschatological fulfillment. "Eschatological" simply means "the end times," which believers still await. Studying these verses in light of these time periods provides believers with a glimpse of God's sovereignty, His complete control over all things, and His omniscience. He knows all things at all times. We can trust what God says, and we can know that we will be the recipients of His blessings past, present, and future.

This passage begins with the Lord saying, "I will pour out my Spirit on all humanity" (Joel 2:28). The nation of Judah, while repentant for the moment, would return to their sinful and rebellious ways. Discipline would come, for they would be exiled and the temple destroyed in the future. But, although discipline would come, God makes a promise to them now. The blessing of His Spirit would

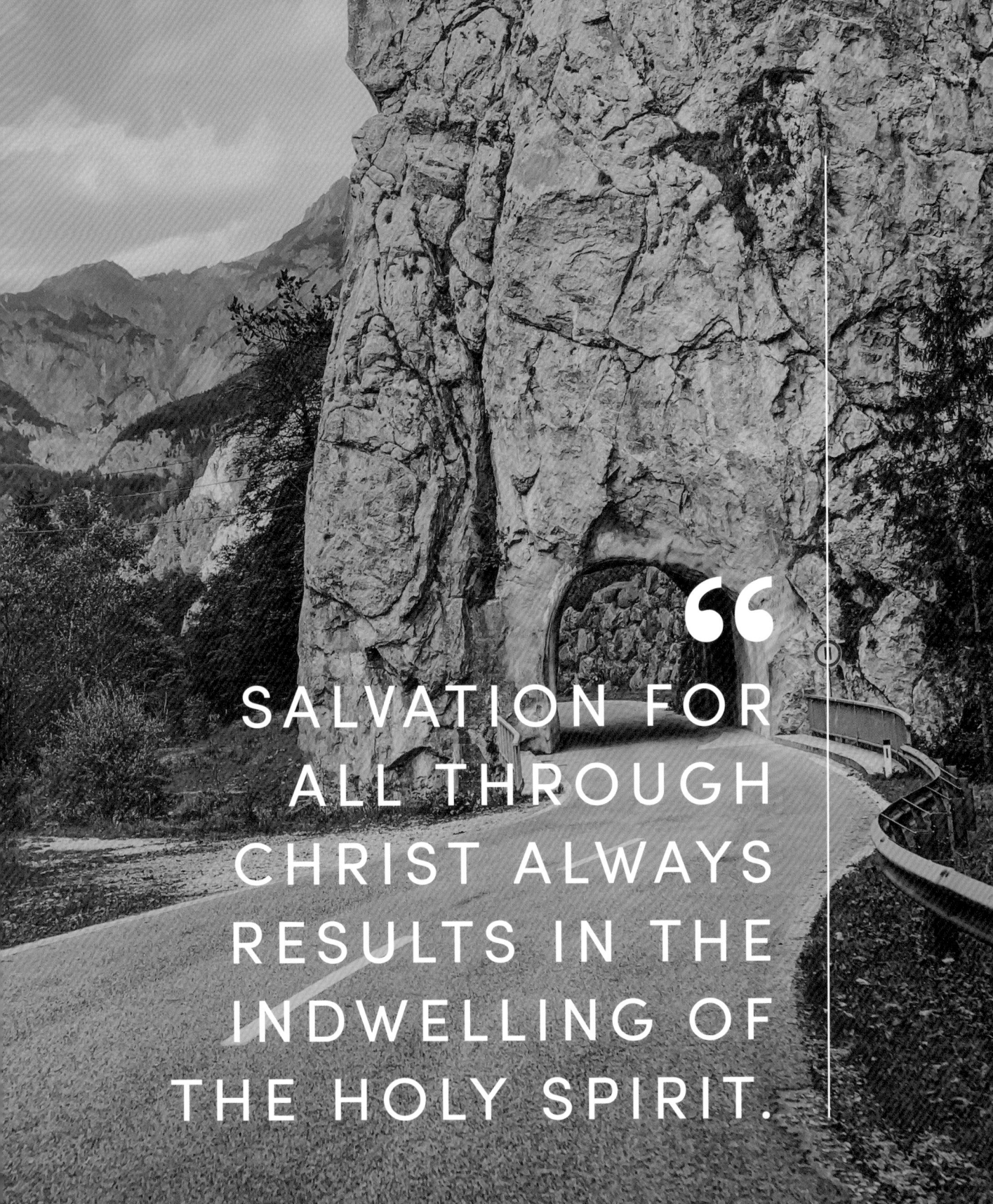

AS WE AWAIT THE DAY JESUS RETURNS FOR US,
WE CAN TRUST THE WORK OF THE SPIRIT IN OUR LIVES.

"

arrive in the future, similar to the blessing He shares through the prophet Ezekiel when He says, "I will give you a new heart and put a new spirit within you; I will remove your heart of stone and give you a heart of flesh" (Ezekiel 36:26). God would not abandon His chosen people, but He also had a plan to include all humanity.

The language used in these verses would have been familiar to the people of Judah. The idea of "pouring out" had long been used to describe God's wrath poured out on the nations or the blood of sacrifices poured out on the altar for Israel's sins. The Spirit would be a continuous expression of God's love freely given to those who follow Him. These verses also speak of wonders displayed in blood, fire, and columns of smoke (Joel 2:30). The nation would have remembered this language from multiple events in its history. Some examples include when Moses turned the Nile River to blood during the first plague on Egypt (Exodus 7:14–25) and the pillar, or column, of smoke and fire that led the Israelites out of Egypt (Exodus 13:17–22). God had been faithful to His people in the past. They could trust Him to pour out His Spirit in the future as He promised.

In the New Testament, once Jesus came, died, resurrected, and ascended into heaven, the promised Spirit was poured out. Now, the Spirit takes a central role in the hearts of those who trust Jesus as their Savior. The Spirit was not only promised by God; Jesus promised it during His earthly ministry, as well. Jesus tells us in John 14:26, "But the Counselor, the Holy Spirit, whom the Father will send in my name, will teach you all things and remind you of everything I have told you." In Acts 2, we see Jesus's disciples awaiting the arrival of the promised Spirit in an upper room. The Spirit then fills the room and rests over the heads of each believer like a tongue of fire. They are then indwelt by the Spirit. God pours out His promised Helper and gives His children a heart of flesh. Led by Peter, they begin speaking the languages of all those gathered in the city.

In his message to the crowd, Peter quotes from Joel 2:28–32. Peter understood the fulfillment of the prophecy spoken by Joel and how all people would be blessed. Through His death, Jesus opened the door for all humanity to be saved. Salvation was not just for the Jew but for the Gentile too (Romans 10:12). God's Spirit was poured out on young, old, male, female, slave, and servant. Paul, who also understood that salvation was for all, even quotes Joel 2:32 in Romans 10:13 when he writes, "For everyone who calls on the name of the Lord will be saved." Salvation for all through Christ always results in the indwelling of the Holy Spirit. The Spirit now fills every believer and leads us to live lives that are a pleasing aroma to the Lord. The promised Spirit in Joel found its fulfillment in the church age.

As an eschatological prophecy, Joel 2:31–32 jumps in time and is a prophecy we still wait to see fulfilled. One day, Jesus will return for His children. At that time, "great and terrible" things will happen. The sun will be dark, the moon will be turned to blood, and the judgment of the Day of the Lord will come. But all those who have called on the name of the Lord Jesus will be saved, and they will dwell with Him in the new heaven and new earth. Believers will be in the presence of Father, Son, and Spirit forever.

These types of prophecies can sometimes be hard to understand or apply. Even though we do not have the complete picture, God does! He has everything under control and has revealed to us all we need to know to love and follow Him. Through salvation in Christ, we now have the promised Spirit. As we await the day Jesus returns for us, we can trust the work of the Spirit in our lives. He leads us to walk in holiness, to be more and more like Jesus. We remain in Him and He in us because of the Spirit (1 John 4:13).

RESPOND

What does this passage teach you about God's character? How does it enable you to trust all of His promises past, present, and future?

RESPOND

The Holy Spirit is poured out on all believers at salvation. If you have accepted Christ, how did you see change in your life when you received salvation and the Spirit, and how have you seen growth since then? If you have not yet received salvation, what questions do you still have about the work of the Spirit?

Read Ephesians 1:13–14, Galatians 5:22–26, and Titus 3:4–7. According to these verses, what is the work of the Spirit in the life of a believer?

NOTES

SCRIPTURE MEMORY

Tear your hearts, not just your clothes, and return to the Lord your God. For he is gracious and compassionate, slow to anger, abounding in faithful love, and he relents from sending disaster.

JOEL 2:13

Practice memorizing this week's Scripture
by writing it out below.

WEEK TWO REFLECTION

REVIEW JOEL 2

01

Paraphrase the passage from this week.

02

What did you observe from this week's text about God and His character?

03

What does this week's passage reveal about the condition of mankind and yourself?

04

How does this passage point to the gospel?

05

How should you respond to this passage? What specific action steps can you take this week to apply this passage?

06

Write a prayer in response to your study of God's Word. Adore God for who He is, confess sins that He revealed in your own life, ask Him to empower you to walk in obedience, and pray for anyone who comes to mind as you study.

WARNING OF FUTURE JUDGMENT

READ JOEL 3:1–3, GENESIS 15

After sharing God's prophecy concerning the coming Spirit, Joel's message will now shift focus. As we saw in our previous study day, there will be a future fulfillment, as well as an eschatological, or end-times, fulfillment regarding these verses. God's message now turns to the nations He will judge for how they treated His chosen people.

God provides multiple reasons for His judgment on these nations in Joel 3:1–8. These first three verses of chapter 3 provide us with the reasons for God's judgment based on the effect that the nations had on His covenant promises. These nations face judgment from God because they committed evil acts against His chosen people. Basically, those who messed with Israel messed with God.

This new chapter starts out hopeful for Judah as God mentions again the restoration He would bring through His mercy and Spirit. While it might be a joyful time for God's people, a message of judgment has arrived for all other sinful nations. Joel shares that the location for these judgments is the Valley of Jehoshaphat. If you look for this valley in a book of biblical maps, you will not find it. This valley, while literal, is symbolically named in this passage. "Jehoshaphat" is translated as "Jehovah has judged." This name of God is to be feared, and the valley where His judgment is poured out will be terrifying.

God brings three charges against these evil nations as reasons for their judgment. First, they scattered Israel to foreign countries. Sec-

IN HIS MERCY AND GRACE,
GOD PROVIDED A WAY FOR ALL PEOPLE TO BE RECONCILED TO HIM.

ond, they divided God's Promised Land, and finally, they sold His people into slavery. These were grievous offenses for various reasons. The Promised Land was very important because of both the physical land it represented and because it was the home of God's chosen people. In His covenant with Abraham, God promised that Abraham's offspring would one day inhabit their own land (Genesis 15). The land was to provide peace and purpose as they worked the land and worshiped God there. These evil nations had scattered the people from their God-ordained home and then divided up the land as spoils of war. God always keeps His covenants, and these nations were not going to thwart His fulfillment. Selling God's people into slavery also showed a blatant disregard for human life. God had called Abraham to be the father of His people. From generation to generation, He told them, "you are a holy people belonging to the Lord your God. The Lord your God has chosen you to be his own possession out of all the peoples on the face of the earth" (Deuteronomy 7:6). Judgment was coming to those who held God's people and His covenants in contempt.

Part of God's judgment on the other nations occurred when the Israelites returned from their exile and resettled in the Promised Land. They rebuilt the temple and the wall, and they once again inhabited the land God gave them (Ezra 6:16–22, Nehemiah 12:27–43). The nations, who had conquered and enslaved them, either ceased to exist or lost the power they once had. Nations like Assyria and Babylon were destroyed, while countries like Egypt still exist today but no longer have dominance over Israel or other counties. God's judgment on these nations occurred thousands of years ago, but His final judgment will be poured out on all nations who do not serve Him during the end times.

The warning of future judgment will also find its fulfillment in the end times. For now, God has withheld His complete wrath. This delay was necessary to bring about God's long-awaited covenant fulfillment through Christ. God's plan was always to save mankind from their sin, both Jew and Gentile. Jesus and His sacrifice on the cross opened the door of salvation—not just to God's chosen people through Abraham but to all people who call on His name. Even Gentiles, or those who are not Jewish, now receive the blessings and promises made to the Israelites. In His sovereign plan, God saves His chosen people and all others who choose to follow Christ. Romans 11:25–26 reminds us, "A partial hardening has come upon Israel until the fullness of the Gentiles has come in. And in this way all Israel will be saved." In His mercy and grace, God provided a way for all people to be reconciled to Him. One day, when Christ returns for His children, God's wrath will consume those nations and peoples who rejected Him. It will be poured out completely, and sin and evil will be purged from the world.

In Christ, believers do not have to fear this final outpouring of wrath. Just like Israel could rest in the promise of restoration in Joel 3:1, so too can Christians rest in the promise that Jesus will one day return for His children. As we wait, though, Jesus gave us a job and purpose. As ambassadors for Christ, we are called to warn others about the coming judgment, just as Joel did in Judah. Colossians 1:28 encourages us in this mission: "We proclaim him, warning and teaching everyone with all wisdom, so that we may present everyone mature in Christ." We seek to proclaim Jesus until the day we take our last breath or He comes in the clouds to take us home. We warn those not in Christ of the tangible punishment that will come for those who do not know Him, yet we make our message not one of complete doom but one of glorious hope and restoration. Yes, Christ takes away the wrath of God in our lives, but more importantly, He gives us abundant life in Him (John 10:10).

RESPOND

How was God faithful to His promises to Abraham? According to Galatians 3:7–9, how are we also recipients of those promises?

RESPOND

Read Jeremiah 25:3–31. According to these verses, God judges all of humanity. What is the result for the wicked? Why can you be assured this will not be your end?

Who do you need to proclaim the gospel to so that they can avoid the coming judgment but, more importantly, have abundant life in Christ? Take some time to write a prayer on behalf of this person. Ask God to give you wisdom and open doors to share the gospel.

NOTES

JUDGMENT ON THE NATIONS

READ JOEL 3:4–8, ISAIAH 23:1–2, EZEKIEL 25:15–17, 2 THESSALONIANS 1:6–9

WEEK 03 / DAY 02

Now that the three major reasons for judgment on these nations have been addressed, Joel moves on to the details of the judgment. Three nations will be specifically called out for what they did to God's people. Retribution, or punishment, has arrived for the crimes these nations committed. This retribution will be historically applicable but also seen in the end times, furthering the eschatological nature of Joel's message.

Through Joel, God specifically addresses three groups of people: Tyre, Sidon, and all the territories of Philistia. Tyre and Sidon are almost always mentioned together as they were both Phoenician cities that sat on the coast of the Mediterranean sea to the north of Judah. Located in modern-day Lebanon, these were seafaring people who trafficked in all types of goods, including slaves. Philistia, also known as the Philistine Pentapolis, was made up of five different cities south of Judah. The majority of the inhabitants were a group of people known as the Philistines, who were long-time enemies of God's people. These three groups bookended God's people and wreaked havoc on their lives for many years.

God's message to these nations begins in Joel 3:4 with two questions: "What are you to me?" and "Are you paying me back or trying to get even with me?" These questions are rhetorical in nature, and the nations' answer to both is a resounding "No." Though powerful in the world, Tyre, Sidon, and Philistia were weak and defenseless against God Almighty. His retribution would come quickly for the

"

AS FOLLOWERS OF CHRIST, WE HAVE A SAVIOR WHO HAS ALREADY CONQUERED EVIL.

AS GOD TOOK CARE OF HIS PROMISED NATION IN THE BOOK OF JOEL,
YOU CAN TRUST HE WILL TAKE CARE OF YOU, TOO.

"

evil done to His people. God then presents more reasons for their punishment. These nations continually plundered Judah. They stole from their houses, and more grievously, they stole from the temple. They took the gold, silver, and finest treasures from God's temple and placed them in the temples of their own gods. Lastly, they sold the people of Judah into slavery. These nations wanted to disperse God's people from the Promised Land and lessen their presence in the region. This was in direct opposition to God's covenant, and He would not allow His people to perish or leave the land promised to Abraham and his descendants.

These verses in Joel give a small glimpse of the retribution paid to these three nations. Their punishment would be the same as what they did to the people of Judah; they would be sold as slaves. God would call back those Judeans who had been scattered, and He would use them to sell the people of Tyre, Sidon, and Philistia to the Sabeans. Also known as the nation of Sheba, the Sabeans were located at the southernmost tip of the Arabian peninsula in modern-day Yemen In other words, these nations would be scattered and dispersed further than the nation of Judah. God's retribution would be complete and greater. Kidnapping was a capital offense under God's law (Deuteronomy 24:7), and these nations would experience the same—but greater—punishment according to God's promise to His people. The Law states, "The Lord your God will put all these curses on your enemies who hate and persecute you" (Deuteronomy 30:7).

Judgment against Tyre, Sidon, and Philistia is found in other places in Scripture. The prophets Isaiah and Ezekiel also spoke of God's punishment of these nations. The prophet Isaiah makes a proclamation against Tyre and Sidon in Isaiah 23:1–2. Both of these strong coastal nations would be destroyed, their ships sunk, and their prosperous trade routes dismantled. The prophet Ezekiel speaks of the Philistines' punishment when God will cut them off and wipe out what remains of their towns (Ezekiel 25:15–17). In the case of each of these prophets, Joel included, there was a historical fulfillment of these punishments, as well as a future fulfillment to come. Each of these nations was indeed destroyed several hundred years before Christ. This was a near fulfillment of the prophecies. One day, these nations will represent those who continually rebel against the Lord, persecute His people, and blaspheme His name. These punishments will come severely and swiftly in the end times as the earth is cleansed from sin and the Lord takes vengeance on His people's behalf.

When Jesus came and died on the cross to save all mankind from sin, He opened the door for all who call on His name to be the recipients of God's covenants and promises. First Peter 2:9–10 reminds us, "But you are a chosen race, a royal priesthood, a holy nation, a people for his possession, so that you may proclaim the praises of the one who called you out of darkness into his marvelous light. Once you were not a people, but now you are God's people; you had not received mercy, but now you have received mercy." Through Jesus, you are one of God's children, and just as He protected Judah, His promised nation, He will protect you.

The idea that we should take vengeance against those who have wronged us is prevalent in our society. Everywhere we look, the idea of an "eye for an eye" is the accepted practice in our culture. But as followers of Christ, we have a Savior who has already conquered evil. No matter who wronged you or what they did, you can trust that God is in control. When the end times come, those who do not know Jesus will be afflicted and pay the penalty for their evil toward God's beloved (2 Thessalonians 1:6–9). God will avenge just as it is written in Romans 12:19, "Friends, do not avenge yourselves; instead, leave room for God's wrath, because it is written, Vengeance belongs to me; I will repay, says the Lord." As God took care of His promised nation in the book of Joel, you can trust He will take care of you, too. Instead of seeking vengeance or growing bitter, pray for those who wrong you. Pray they will come to know Jesus as their Savior and experience the beautiful gift of restoration.

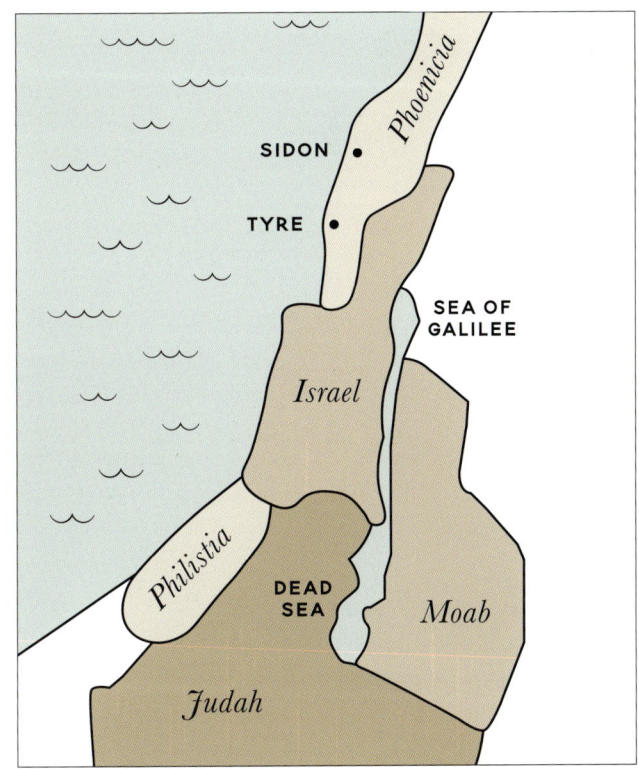

RESPOND

Tyre, Sidon, and Philistia represent all people who oppose God. How do people in our society today oppose God? What sins are prevalent? How are followers of Christ treated?

How did Christ take ultimate vengeance on sin, death, and evil? Why can you trust that He will avenge all wrongs past, present, and future?

Read the following verses: Deuteronomy 32:35, Psalm 21:11, and Romans 12:17–21. When you are tempted to seek vengeance, how can these verses remind you God is in control? How are believers called to treat their enemies?

NOTES

JUDGMENT PROCLAIMED

READ JOEL 3:9–16, 2 PETER 3:10–18, REVELATION 14:14–20

WEEK 03 / DAY 03

The stage has been set, and the nations have been warned: God's judgment is coming. The next several verses of Joel play out like a movie script for the end times still to come—the scene is described, the characters are named, and the action is explained. The Day of the Lord is upon the nations in this passage. While it is a fearsome and terrible day, Israel and those in Christ can have hope and trust in God Almighty as their eternal refuge.

On this future Day of the Lord, the promised vengeance on the nations arrives, and God proclaims that the nations must prepare for holy war. Holy war in Scripture typically refers to annihilation. This is not just a small battle over land or kingdoms; this is the ultimate battle between the nations and God. In Joel 3:9–10, the armies are told to assemble and prepare by turning their farming tools into weapons. Those who are weak are even called to battle. These nations, which God once used to bring discipline to His own people during their exile, will now face God's wrath for their wickedness. They are called to fight, but they cannot win against the Lord of Armies. In Psalm 24:8, the psalmist reminds us of this truth: "Who is this King of glory? The Lord, strong and mighty, the Lord, mighty in battle."

The place of the Lord's judgment was first named in Joel 3:2 and is repeated here in verse 12. The nations will come to the Valley of Jehoshaphat to be judged. The Valley of Jehoshaphat is not the literal name of a known valley. However, as discussed a couple of

"IN THE BIBLE, GOD HAS GIVEN US EVERYTHING WE NEED TO LIVE OUR LIVES FOR HIS GLORY.

PROCLAIM LIFE THROUGH JESUS, AND
LOOK FORWARD TO THE DAY WHEN YOU WILL LIVE IN HIS LIGHT FOREVER.

> days ago, Jehoshaphat means "Jehovah has judged." So the name of this valley likely refers to the place where God carries out His judgment on the nations.

In this portion of the prophecy, agricultural language is used to describe how the harvest of the wicked is ripe. In the book of Revelation, the Apostle John sees a similar scene in which the Son of Man and an angel each have a sickle to harvest the evil of the earth: "So the angel swung his sickle at the earth and gathered the grapes from the vineyard of the earth, and he threw them into the great winepress of God's wrath" (Revelation 14:19). Sin has consumed God's creation. One day, His wrath will be poured out on the earth, and those who do not know and fear the Lord will experience God's terrible punishment.

Multitudes will be drawn to the valley of judgment. The day of decision will be marked by the darkening of the sun, moon, and stars. Old Testament prophets like Joel, Isaiah, and Ezekiel each speak of this phenomenon on the day of judgment. Ezekiel, speaking on God's behalf, says, "'When I snuff you out, I will cover the heavens and darken their stars. I will cover the sun with a cloud, and the moon will not give its light'" (Ezekiel 32:7). God alone is the source of all light, and on that dark day of judgment, it is only fitting that the sources of light all mankind placed their trust in would cease their shining. The nations will bow before the true Light.

On that day, the Lord will roar, and heaven and earth will shake. Judgment will come swiftly to the wicked. The proclamation could end there, but God in His great mercy reminds Israel they have nothing to fear. They have been restored to a right relationship with Him, and He will be their refuge and stronghold. When Jesus came and died on the cross, He bore the wrath of God on our behalf. On that day, the sky darkened as the light of the world was snuffed out because of our sin (Luke 23:44). But on that first resurrection Sunday, His light shone brightly as He conquered sin and death. When we call on His name for salvation, we can trust that we no longer await punishment and judgment from God. We have been restored and grafted into every promise and covenant God made to His chosen people. We will one day dwell in His presence for eternity where no light will be needed because He will be the light (Revelation 22:5).

As we await that glorious day, what do we do? How should we live? In the Bible, God has given us everything we need to live our lives for His glory. Jesus gave us a job and a purpose to share the gospel with everyone (Matthew 28:18–20). And Peter tells us, "while you wait for these things, make every effort to be found without spot or blemish in his sight, at peace. . . . grow in the grace and knowledge of our Lord and Savior Jesus Christ" (2 Peter 3:14, 18). You can rest safely in your Savior's arms as you grow in Christlikeness and fulfill His mission for your life. He is your refuge and stronghold. Proclaim life through Jesus, and look forward to the day when you will live in His light forever.

RESPOND

How do you see wickedness in our world today? Why is God just and right to punish sin?

RESPOND

While believers are thankful they will not experience this terrible future wrath, our hearts must be concerned for those who do not know Christ. Write down a few names of people you believe do not know Jesus. Spend some time praying for their salvation.

Read Psalm 62:5–8. How do these verses further encourage you that God is your refuge and stronghold? Write a prayer of thanksgiving that Christ has restored you to a right relationship with God and you do not have to face His wrath. If you have not yet accepted the Lord as your Savior, consider doing so today. He is ready and waiting for you to come to Him.

NOTES

THE LORD DWELLS IN ZION

READ JOEL 3:17–21, JEREMIAH 31:31–34, REVELATION 21:1–8, 21:22–22:5

Joel's prophetic message to the nation of Judah is drawing to a close. These final verses point them, and us, to a time of future fulfillment we still await. In those days, God will declare judgment on the evil nations and end the dark, barren days of the past for His people. Hope eternal will reign. Judgment will be no more, and God's chosen people will flourish again in His presence. God will once again dwell with His people as He always planned.

Joel 3:17 reminds Judah that all people will know God is Lord over all—those who are judged and those who are saved. He will dwell in Zion on His holy mountain. This is the sixth time the word "Zion" has been used so far in Joel, and each time, it represents the very presence of God with His people. His presence purifies Jerusalem and makes it a city where only His people will worship Him forever.

On that great and glorious day, God will bring complete restoration to His people and to His creation. Everything the locusts destroyed will once again be abundant in God's presence. The harvest will be plentiful, and all droughts will cease. A spring will come from the Lord's house in Jerusalem to water the valley. Joel mentions the Valley of Acacias in these verses. Like the Valley of Jehoshaphat, this valley is not found on any maps. However, Jerusalem is surrounded by many valleys, and acacia trees were known to grow in the dry and infertile soil of these valleys. Joel's description would have made complete sense to the farming nation of Judah. While

" ON THAT GREAT AND GLORIOUS DAY, GOD WILL BRING COMPLETE RESTORATION TO HIS PEOPLE AND TO HIS CREATION.

> ## THROUGH THE SINLESS SACRIFICE OF JESUS,
> ### ALL THOSE WHO CALL ON HIS NAME ARE SAVED.

we may not know the exact location of the Valley of Acacias, we can trust that wherever its location lies, the spring will turn dry and infertile soil to life in God's presence forever.

Two more enemy nations of Israel receive judgment in this passage: Egypt and Edom. Both nations had long hated Israel and plundered and destroyed her cities and her people. These nations will be physically destroyed, but they also represent all people who oppose God. Those who oppose God are His enemies, and they will feel the wrath of His judgment. In the end, these nations and those who oppose God will become a wasteland, a direct contrast to the abundant and flourishing city of Jerusalem ruled by God.

The contrast to these desolate nations continues when God declares unending security for His people. Jerusalem will be inhabited forever from generation to generation. Those of us who live on this side of Christ's first coming have the gift of further explanation in the book of Revelation. In his vision of the end times, the Apostle John seemingly takes the words shared by Joel and paints a bigger, more glorious picture. The new heaven and new earth will be filled with the presence of God. His glory will be the only light needed, the only temple where worship will take place, and the spring of the water of life (Revelation 21:6, 21:22, 21:23). John tells us in Revelation 22:1–3, "Then he showed me the river of the water of life, clear as crystal, flowing from the throne of God and of the Lamb down the middle of the city's main street. The tree of life was on each side of the river, bearing twelve kinds of fruit, producing its fruit every month. The leaves of the tree are for healing the nations, and there will no longer be any curse. The throne of God and of the Lamb will be in the city, and his servants will worship him." The harvest will be abundant and eternal. The locusts of sin will no longer destroy, and God's children will worship in His presence for eternity.

The beauty and fullness of God's character are on display in the final verse of Joel. We get a glimpse of His just and merciful nature. The bloodguilt of the nation, which had not been completely pardoned yet, points to the need for a coming Savior. We are reminded that judgment is required for sin. But, in His perfect timing, God would provide the final sacrifice needed to end all sin. Through the sinless sacrifice of Jesus, all those who call on His name are saved. Forgiveness and pardon are provided. Through the prophet Jeremiah, God tells His children, "For I will forgive their iniquity and never again remember their sin" (Jeremiah 31:34). The covenant God made with His people in Jeremiah says not only will He forgive their iniquity, but He will put His teaching in them and write it on their hearts. He will be their God, and they will be His people (Jeremiah 31:33). Jesus provides us with new hearts—hearts that desire to serve the Lord, love His commands, and love others (1 John 5:1–2). With our new, pardoned hearts through Jesus, we look forward to the day we will dwell in Zion with our God.

Through Joel, God has painted a beautiful picture of Himself for us. Throughout this prophetic message, we have seen how both judgment and salvation point to the knowledge of God and His covenants. They point to our need for a Savior and restoration to our God. As we await the day when Christ returns, we have work to do. Jesus gave us a new heart and a new spirit, and the correct response is to worship Him, live our lives for Him, and tell others about Him. The locusts of life may seek to destroy, but trust in your God who brought restoration to your life through salvation. Live with hope, for the Lord restores, and one day you will dwell with Him in Zion.

RESPOND

How have you seen both judgment and restoration throughout Joel? As you await complete restoration, what do you look forward to the most when you will dwell in Zion with the Lord?

RESPOND

In the last five verses of Joel, we read that the Lord will dwell in Zion. Read John 17:20–23. How does Jesus enable us to dwell with the Father now and in the future? Now read John 16:7–14. How does the Holy Spirit enable you to live in God's presence now as you await Christ's return?

Take a look back at page 21 to reread your response to the very first question on Week 1 Day 1. Based on your answer, how have you grown in your understanding of Joel? Were your questions answered? How can the lessons you learned in Joel help you move forward and study other prophetic books of the Bible?

NOTES

GOD'S CHARACTER IN JOEL

READ JOEL 1–3

The book of Joel has come to a close. Throughout this small prophetic message, two major themes lived side by side: judgment and restoration. God is the author and perfecter of both. While these may be two major attributes of God, Joel displays many others in just seventy-three verses. Take some time to read all three chapters of Joel one more time. As you read, focus on where you see God's attributes. Then, use the chart on page 112 to record what attribute(s) you see in each of the verses listed, followed by how you see that attribute displayed. (See page 6 for a list and descriptions of God's attributes.)

We hope this study reminds you that all Scripture is about God and His glory. The Bible is filled with many mysteries, and we do not have all the answers, but God never intended for us to have them. When we do not have all the answers, we must rely on Him and seek Him with our whole hearts.

Joel taught us that judgment will come. But he also taught us that we have a God who brings restoration to His children. Jesus restores us to a right relationship with God. Jesus restores us to be the images-bearers God intended us to be. And Jesus will restore us to the presence of the Father when He returns for us again. As the Apostle Paul says, "Thanks be to God for his indescribable gift" (2 Corinthians 9:15)! In Christ, we can trust that the Lord restores.

> "ALL SCRIPTURE IS ABOUT GOD AND HIS GLORY.

VERSE(S)	ATTRIBUTE(S) OF GOD	HOW THIS ATTRIBUTE IS DISPLAYED
JOEL 1:1		
JOEL 1:15		
JOEL 2:1		
JOEL 2:11		
JOEL 2:13		
JOEL 2:18		
JOEL 2:26		
JOEL 2:32		
JOEL 3:12		
JOEL 3:16		
JOEL 3:20–21		

NOTES

SCRIPTURE MEMORY

Then I heard a loud voice from the throne: Look, God's dwelling is with humanity, and he will live with them. They will be his peoples, and God himself will be with them and will be their God.

Revelation 21:3

Practice memorizing this week's Scripture by writing it out below.

WEEK THREE REFLECTION

REVIEW JOEL 3

01

Paraphrase the passage from this week.

02

What did you observe from this week's text about God and His character?

03

What does this week's passage reveal about the condition of mankind and yourself?

04

How does this passage point to the gospel?

05

How should you respond to this passage? What specific action steps can you take this week to apply this passage?

06

Write a prayer in response to your study of God's Word. Adore God for who He is, confess sins that He revealed in your own life, ask Him to empower you to walk in obedience, and pray for anyone who comes to mind as you study.

WHAT IS THE GOSPEL?

THANK YOU FOR READING AND ENJOYING THIS STUDY WITH US! WE ARE ABUNDANTLY GRATEFUL FOR THE WORD OF GOD, THE INSTRUCTION WE GLEAN FROM IT, AND THE EVER-GROWING UNDERSTANDING IT PROVIDES FOR US OF GOD'S CHARACTER. WE ARE ALSO THANKFUL THAT SCRIPTURE CONTINUALLY POINTS TO ONE THING IN INNUMERABLE WAYS: THE GOSPEL.

We remember our brokenness when we read about the fall of Adam and Eve in the garden of Eden (Genesis 3), where sin entered into a perfect world and maimed it. We remember the necessity that something innocent must die to pay for our sin when we read about the atoning sacrifices in the Old Testament. We read that we have all sinned and fallen short of the glory of God (Romans 3:23) and that the penalty for our brokenness, the wages of our sin, is death (Romans 6:23). We all need grace and mercy, but most importantly, we all need a Savior.

We consider the goodness of God when we realize that He did not plan to leave us in this dire state. We see His promise to buy us back from the clutches of sin and death in Genesis 3:15. And we see that promise accomplished with Jesus Christ on the cross. Jesus Christ knew no sin yet became sin so that we might become righteous through His sacrifice (2 Corinthians 5:21). Jesus was tempted in every way that we are and lived sinlessly. He was reviled yet still yielded Himself for our sake, that we may have life abundant in Him. Jesus lived the perfect life that we could not live and died the death that we deserved.

The gospel is profound yet simple. There are many mysteries in it that we will never understand this side of heaven, but there is still overwhelming weight to its implications in this life. The gospel tells of our sinfulness and God's goodness and a gracious gift that compels a response. We are saved by grace through faith, which means that we rest with

faith in the grace that Jesus Christ displayed on the cross (Ephesians 2:8-9). We cannot save ourselves from our brokenness or do any amount of good works to merit God's favor. Still, we can have faith that what Jesus accomplished in His death, burial, and resurrection was more than enough for our salvation and our eternal delight. When we accept God, we are commanded to die to ourselves and our sinful desires and live a life worthy of the calling we have received (Ephesians 4:1). The gospel compels us to be sanctified, and in so doing, we are conformed to the likeness of Christ Himself. This is hope. This is redemption. This is the gospel.

SCRIPTURES TO REFERENCE:

GENESIS 3:15	*I will put hostility between you and the woman, and between your offspring and her offspring. He will strike your head, and you will strike his heel.*
ROMANS 3:23	*For all have sinned and fall short of the glory of God.*
ROMANS 6:23	*For the wages of sin is death, but the gift of God is eternal life in Christ Jesus our Lord.*
2 CORINTHIANS 5:21	*He made the one who did not know sin to be sin for us, so that in him we might become the righteousness of God.*
EPHESIANS 2:8-9	*For you are saved by grace through faith, and this is not from yourselves; it is God's gift — not from works, so that no one can boast.*
EPHESIANS 4:1-3	*Therefore I, the prisoner in the Lord, urge you to walk worthy of the calling you have received, with all humility and gentleness, with patience, bearing with one another in love, making every effort to keep the unity of the Spirit through the bond of peace.*

Thank you for studying
God's Word with us!

CONNECT WITH US
@thedailygraceco
@dailygracepodcast

CONTACT US
info@thedailygraceco.com

SHARE
#thedailygraceco

VISIT US ONLINE
www.thedailygraceco.com

MORE DAILY GRACE
The Daily Grace App
Daily Grace Podcast